Addison-Wesley
science

Verne N. Rockcastle   Betty J. McKnight   Frank R. Salamon   Victor E. Schmidt

Addison-Wesley Publishing Company

Menlo Park, California   Reading, Massachusetts   London   Amsterdam   Don Mills, Ontario   Sydney

Photo Credits

Andree Abecassis*: 11 L, 13 C, 17, 19, 27, 28 B, 33 BL, 33 BR, 41, 45, 48 R, 52 R, 53 R, 53 L, 55, 57, 59 L, 67, 70, 75, 77, 85 TR, 91 CR, 92, 93, 94 TR, 95, 97, 99 107, 108, 112 BR, 116, 117, 119, 135, 140, 141 L, 142, 143, 146, 159, 160, 162, 176, 177 L, 195, 200; Jen & Des Bartlett/ Bruce Coleman Inc.: 18 BL; W. Bayer/Bruce Coleman Inc.: 214 B; Elihu Blotnick*: 18 T; Elihu Blotnick © 1978: 130 BR, 156 B, 219 B; John M. Burnley: 204 L; Jane Burton/ Bruce Coleman Inc.: 29 TL; California Academy of Sciences, UPI Franklin Institute: 147; Raymond Coleman/Tom Stack & Associates: 217 CL; Dr. W. Aubrey Crich: 204 TR; Thase Daniel/Bruce Coleman Inc.: 18 BR; Jack Dermid/Bruce Coleman Inc.: 205 TL; William Eastman/Tom Stack & Associates: 219 C; Robert Evans/Tom Stack & Associates: 13 R; Breck P. Kent/ Animals, Animals: 23, 24; Breck P. Kent/Earth Scenes: 31, 112 BL; Earl Kubis/Tom Stack & Associates: 217 BL; Wayland Lee*/Addison-Wesley Publishing Company: 184; J. Markham/ Bruce Coleman Inc.: 29 BC; Betty McKnight: 13 L; Gary Meszaros/ Bruce Coleman Inc.: 21; Gary Milburn/Tom Stack & Associates: 219 T; Robert Mitchell/Tom Stack & Associates: 29 BL; NASA: 154 T, 154 B; Pat North: 11 BR; R. E. Pelham/Bruce Coleman Inc.: 214 T; Publishers Graphics*: 23, 31 R, 83, 96, 163, 169, 181, 198; Verne N. Rockcastle: 4–5, 6, 12 L, 12 R, 20, 28 T, 29 BR, 32–33, 34, 123, 196, 197, 205 CL, 210, 213 TL, 213 TC; Leonard L. Rue III/Animals, Animals: 217 TR; Leonard L. Rue III/Bruce Coleman Inc.: 29 TR; Leonard L. Rue III/ Tom Stack & Associates: 214 C; R. Hamilton Smith/Photo Library: 96; Tom Stack/ Tom Stack & Associates: 177 R, 205 BR, 220; L. D. Topoleski: 205 BL; United States Geological Survey: 49; R. Williams/Earth Scenes: 165; Yerkes Observatory Photo: 175.

*Photographs provided expressly for the publisher
All other photographs by Addison-Wesley staff

Cover: Soap bubbles
Illustration by D.J. Simison/Dow, Clement & Simison

Illustrators

Lee Ames
Robert Bausch
Emily Chronic
Dick Cole
Jean Helmer
Susan Jaekel
Heather King
Jim LaMarche
Dennis Nolan
Publishers Graphics
Norman Nicholson
Margaret Sanfilippo
Ed Taber
Al Wiseman

ISBN 0-201-11863-7
   DEFGHIJKL-VH-898765

Contents

Once this log was part of a living plant. In time, the log breaks into bits. It *decays*. Tiny plants, small animals, and water help the log to decay. Roots of the plants open spaces in the wood. Small animals chew holes in the log.

The plants, animals, and water all *interact*. In time, the log disappears. It becomes part of the soil. From the soil new plants will grow.

Sun, Water, Soil, and Air

The sun is important to living things. So is water. So are soil and air. What is soil? Why is it important?

Different kinds of soil. Sometimes settlers named their towns after the kinds of soil they found there. What do you think the soil is like in Sandy, Oregon? What color do you think the soil is in Red Rock, Texas, or Black Earth, Wisconsin? What kind of soil could you find in Gravel Point, Ontario?

Soil comes in many different colors. It can be fine, like flour, or gritty, like sand. The soil in Rocky Comfort, Missouri, might be full of small stones and pebbles.

What color is the soil where you live? If you wanted to name your town after the kind of soil that is found there, what would you call it?

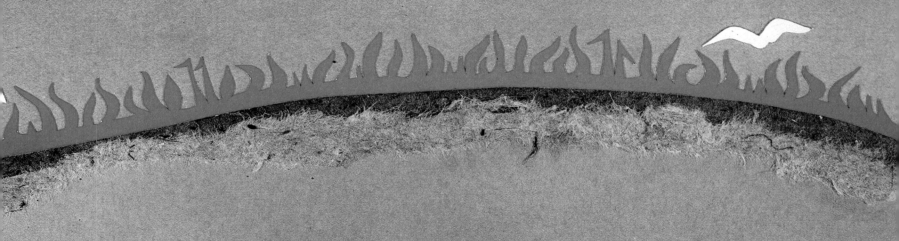

Soil is a mixture.   Most soil is a mixture of
- bits of rock
- bits of decayed plant and animal matter
- water

Green plants need soil chemicals. They use these chemicals when making leaves, stems, and roots.

Aphids eat leaves. Do aphids *depend* on soil? A ladybug eats aphids. Do ladybugs depend on soil?

Some plants make corn. Corn plants need water and soil chemicals. Mice eat corn. Some snakes eat mice. Do the snakes depend on soil?

Plants grow in different kinds of soil. Some soil is hard and dry. Some is soft and wet. Could some soil be better than others for plants? How could you find out?

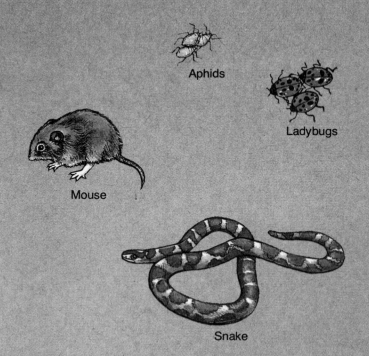

Aphids

Ladybugs

Mouse

Snake

7

A good experiment must be a *fair test.* That means testing only one thing at a time.

Suppose you want to find out how plants grow in different soils. You should keep these things the same

- kind of seed
- amount of light
- temperature
- amount of water

Only the soil will be different.

Suppose all the plants don't grow the same. Then you will know the soil made the difference because the seeds, light, and water were kept the same.

Put three cups of sand in a wide-mouth jar. Rinse the sand with water, pouring off the water slowly. Do this until the water is clear.

Do not pour this water down the sink! Why?

When the sand is clean, spread it out to dry. Stir the sand from time to time. Then it will dry faster.

Now get four paper cups. Make four small holes in the bottom of each cup as shown. Fill cups 1, 2, and 3 with sand. Fill cup 4 with lawn soil. Put grass cuttings in cup 2. Put plant food in cup 3.

Plant four radish seeds in each cup. Push the seeds one centimetre (1 cm) under the soil.

Put each cup on a small plate. Then put all the cups where they will get the same amount of sunlight. Water each cup every day. Use the same amount of water for each cup.

Keep records with dates and drawings during the next three weeks.

SOME QUESTIONS TO THINK ABOUT

1. In which cup did the seeds grow best?

2. Which cup seemed to have had the fewest chemicals?

3. Did the seeds begin to grow in the sand with no plant food? Why might this have happened?

4. Why did you have to keep these the same

- cups?
- water?
- seeds?
- light?

Was this a fair test? Was it a good experiment?

Air, too, is a mixture. Air is a mixture of gases. Two of them are *oxygen* and *carbon dioxide*.

All animals, large and small, need oxygen to live. You use oxygen for growing, moving, and even for thinking. Your body needs oxygen for everything it does. When you breathe in, you take in some oxygen. When you breathe out, you give off some carbon dioxide.

Plants also need oxygen. Like animals, plants use oxygen to grow. Plants use oxygen to produce flowers and seeds. Nearly all living things use oxygen and give off carbon dioxide.

Suppose that living things kept using oxygen for a long time. Suppose, too, that the oxygen they used was never replaced. What do you think would happen in time?

Producing food and oxygen. Elodea is a green water plant used in many aquariums. If you have ever looked at any elodea, you may have seen tiny bubbles on the leaves. These are bubbles of oxygen. They come from a *chemical action* in the plant. This chemical action makes food for the plant. It also gives off oxygen. In this way green plants replace the oxygen used by living things.

Green plants make food from carbon dioxide and water. This takes energy. Green plants get the energy mostly from sunlight. Plants can even get energy from electric lights.

Green plants put back oxygen into the air. They put back more oxygen than they use. Some of this oxygen is used by animals. This is one way that plants and animals interact.

Green plants growing on land are not the only things that give off oxygen. In the ocean are millions of plants that most people never see. These plants also give off oxygen. What would the world be like if green plants did not put back oxygen into the air?

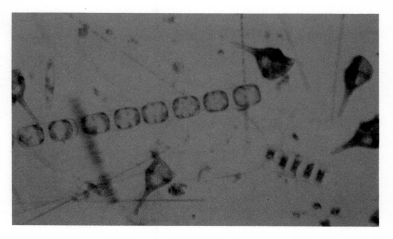

A Lawn Community LESSON 2

Find a grassy place. It could be a park. It could be on the school lawn. Or it could be in your own yard. Look down between the plants. Look for anything that moves. What kinds of animals can you find? What kinds of plants? How might these plants and animals interact?

The plants and animals that live together in a certain place form a *community*. A community is a group of living things that live together and interact. Sometimes a community can be very small. Sometimes it can be large. A park is a community. A lawn is a community.

Honeybee

Toad

What is a lawn? Did you ever walk across a lawn? Play on a lawn? Keep off a lawn?

What is a lawn? To many people it is a grassy place. It has few weeds. Was grass the only kind of plant you found? Were there spiders, insects, and earthworms living there?

Could you have a lawn community without grass? What might it be like without insects or earthworms? Do you know that earthworms make holes, eat dead leaves, and mix the soil?

To take away one kind of plant or animal might change the whole community.

Earthworm

Slug

Dandelion

SOMETHING TO TRY

Imagine a sample of lawn 30 cm wide, 30 cm long, and 8 cm deep. How many kinds of plants and animals would it have? Write your *prediction.* Then test it.

First, get permission to dig up a sample of lawn. Dig down 8 cm. Then lift out the sample.

Put it in a large bag and take it to your classroom. Spread newspapers on the floor. Then divide the sample into smaller samples.

Carefully take each smaller sample apart. Look for plants that are not grass. Use a magnifying glass to search for tiny animals. Record what you find.

PLANTS	ANIMALS
grass ||||| ||||| ||||	earthworm |||
dandelion ||	ants ||||| ||||
buttercup		spider |||
clover ||	snail ||
unknown ||||| ||	beetle	
	centipede	
	unknown ||||| ||

Make a class list of what was found. Are you surprised that so many animals lived in this sample? Did you find any that you had never seen before?

When you are finished, take your lawn sample back. Use it to fill the hole in the lawn. Always return living things that you borrow.

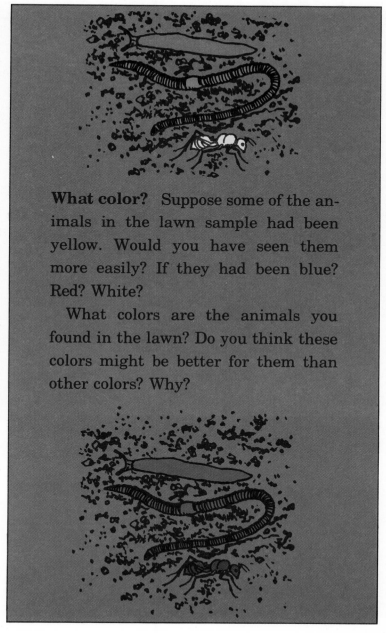

What color? Suppose some of the animals in the lawn sample had been yellow. Would you have seen them more easily? If they had been blue? Red? White?

What colors are the animals you found in the lawn? Do you think these colors might be better for them than other colors? Why?

Matching moths. Long ago, a certain kind of moth lived in England. Over time, scientists discovered that the moth had developed into two groups. One group was light-colored. It lived on light, clean trees in the country. The other group was dark-colored. It lived on darker, dirtier trees in the city.

A scientist named Ford thought that birds might be able to find and eat the dark moths if they lived in the country. He thought that birds might be able to find and eat the light moths if they lived in the city.

A scientist named Kettlewell checked Ford's idea. He released dark moths in the country. He released light moths in the city.

Which moths do you think were eaten by birds?

Which moths do you think lived to produce more moths in the country? Which lived to produce more moths in the city?

SOMETHING TO THINK ABOUT

Suppose earthworms came in all colors. Suppose the young earthworms were always the same color as their parents. Which color of earthworms would probably escape their enemies? Which color would probably live and produce more of their own kind?

A lawn community is not simple. In your lawn sample, did you find more kinds of living things than you predicted? A lawn community is not simple. It contains more living things than most people think. These living things depend on each other, or interact, in many ways.

Grass and other green plants in the lawn make food. They also give off oxygen. They make food from carbon dioxide and water, using energy from sunlight. Energy is stored in this food. When animals eat plants, they get this energy.

Interactions. Green plants make and store food. Earthworms, slugs, and snails eat parts of green plants. When they eat plants, they eat some of this stored food. Would you say that, in a way, they get energy from the sun? Why do you think so?

In what other ways do earthworms interact with plants? Earthworms make holes in the soil. In making holes, the worms mix and loosen the soil. Plants grow more easily in this kind of soil. Why?

How do earthworms interact with other animals such as birds?

17

A Desert Community LESSON 3

It doesn't rain very often in a desert. Also, the temperature may change from very hot in the daytime to near freezing at night. Yet many plants and animals may live there.

Cactus plants are members of some desert communities. Most cactus plants have thick stems with a waxlike covering. The plants store water in these stems. The covering slows down the water loss of the plant.

Desert animals also have special ways to live there. Many rest during the hot, dry days. They may lie in the shade of plants. Or, under rocks. Or, in holes. Most desert animals move about only at night.

Some desert animals get water by eating plants. One animal, the pocket mouse, produces water from the seeds it eats.

Insects are also part of a desert community. Some feed on desert plants. Then spiders, lizards, and mice feed on these insects. Snakes, owls, coyotes, and hawks feed on the spiders, lizards, and mice. Animals that hunt are hunted. Living things in a desert interact in many ways.

Desert plants. The children in the picture are looking at plants in a desert *terrarium*. It is like a model of the desert. The plants are growing in sand. The children water them only about twice a week. The water drains through the sand into the stones at the bottom. You can find plants for a desert terrarium in most plant stores. They are called *succulents*. Succulents often have smooth, thick leaves and stems. They can hold lots of water so that they can live in dry places. Prickly succulents are called *cactus* plants. Many kinds of cactus plants have beautiful, bright flowers when they bloom in the spring.

19

A Pond Community LESSON 4

Have you ever watched a pond in spring? Or fished in one in summer? A pond may seem to be a quiet place, but is it, really?

Insects fly near the water or scoot over its surface. Small water animals swim there. They move between the stems of plants. They crawl under floating leaves. Other animals move among the plant roots. Many things are happening!

Life in a pond. A pond community has many living things in it. There are water plants and fish. These spend their whole lives in the pond. There also are frogs, turtles, and insects. These may spend only part of their lives in the pond.

Dragonfly nymph   Damselfly nymph   Diving beetle

Giant waterbug   Mayfly nymph   Water strider

Many land animals also belong to the pond community. But some get only their feet wet!

What members of a pond community can you name?

The living things in the pond community interact with each other. They interact with the water, soil, and air, too.

In the pond, some of the larger animals feed on smaller ones. Others feed on water plants. Some fish feed on insects. Frogs, fish, and water plants often become food for animals outside the water. Look carefully at the animals in the picture. Can you tell where each gets its food?

Protection. Water protects many pond animals from being caught and eaten by other animals. It is hard for land animals to see very far into the water. They cannot see animals hiding among the plants or on the bottom. Land animals cannot smell pond animals in the water.

Water also protects the things living in it from quick temperature changes. Water temperature does not change as fast as air temperature.

Get two large jars. Place a thermometer in each. Fill one jar with water. Let both jars stand until the temperatures inside them are the same.

Now put both jars in a refrigerator. Leave them for 15 minutes. Check each thermometer. In which jar is the temperature lower?

"Fenced in." Water helps to protect many members of a pond community. But some of those that need to live in water are "fenced in." They cannot leave the water. If a pond dries up, they may die. They cannot move to another pond.

If a woodchuck's home is dug up, it can move to another field. When a deer is in danger, it can run away. Pond animals such as frogs and turtles can get away. They can move to another pond. But many animals cannot. They are "fenced in."

How do water animals get oxygen? Even animals that live in water must have oxygen. Without it, they would die.

Oxygen used by water animals and plants comes mostly from
- the air above the water
- the water plants

Turtles and frogs come to the surface of the water to breathe. They have lungs, as you do. They must breathe air.

Some water animals get air through tubes. Young mosquitoes do this. Mosquito eggs *hatch* into little "wigglers." These are called *larvae*.

When the larvae need air, they come to the surface. Each larva takes in air through a tube at the tail.

Many water animals, however, do not have to come to the surface to get air. Instead, they use oxygen that is *dissolved* in water. They get this oxygen through *gills*. Both fish and tadpoles have gills. Some water insects have gills, too.

The dissolved oxygen cannot be seen. Where does it come from? Some of it comes from the air above the pond. But much of it comes from green water plants. Much of this oxygen dissolves and mixes with the water.

Breathing tube

Mosquito larva

A pond in winter. In winter, many pond plants die. Fewer plants means less oxygen for the animals that live there. Also, ice may cover the pond. Then not much air gets into the water.

Many animals spend winter in the mud at the bottom of the pond. They are not very active. Thus, they don't need much food or oxygen. That is how they live through winter.

Some water animals die when winter comes. But before they die, they lay eggs. The eggs last through winter. When spring comes, young animals hatch out.

SOMETHING TO FIND OUT

Try to find out how the following insects spend the winter:

- a dragonfly
- a mosquito
- a water strider

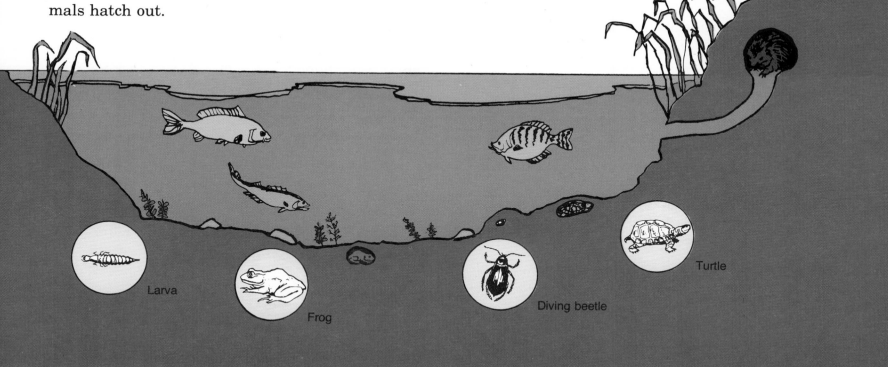

Larva

Frog

Diving beetle

Turtle

Borrow a pond sample. The pond may be close to a city building, in a park, or in the country. Ask if you may borrow a few plants and animals from it for a few days.

When you go to the pond, take these things with you

- a container with a lid
- a white dish or bowl
- a strainer

Fill the container about half full with pond water. Add a few water plants. Then add a little material from the bottom of the pond.

With the strainer, scoop up some mud near the edge. Most pond animals live near the edge. Dump this material into the dish. Watch for something that wiggles. If it looks interesting, put it in your container.

When you have four or five animals, STOP! Don't put in any more, unless you take out some. Each animal must have enough oxygen to live.

After you have the animals you want, put the lid on the container.

After you bring your pond sample home, take the lid off. Put the container where it will get light, but not direct sunlight.

Use a magnifying glass to watch the life in your container. To look closely at something, put it in a small dish of pond water. As you look, ask yourself

- How does it get oxygen?
- How does it get food?
- What does it eat?
- Does anything eat it?
- Does it move around? If so, how?
- How might it have spent the winter?

Remember—after a few days, return the pond sample. You only *borrowed* it!

A Vacant Lot Community LESSON 5

A lot is often called *vacant* if it has no building on it. But is a vacant lot really vacant or empty? Not at all! It may have lots of interesting things in it. It may have car bodies, tires, cans, and pieces of cardboard.

What else can you find in a vacant lot? Could a vacant lot be a community just as a lawn is?

27

Visiting a vacant lot. A lawn is mostly grass. But a vacant lot may have mostly weeds. Or, it may be nearly bare. When it is bare, the sun can make the soil warm and dry.

Many small animals cannot live in a warm, dry place. They need cool, moist places. Sometimes a vacant lot has cool, moist places. Where do you think these could be?

What animals can you find under flat objects in a vacant lot? Look under old pieces of cardboard and wood. Lift them up carefully. Are there any small animals that are gray and have many legs? Some of these may roll into little balls. These are pill bugs. Otherwise, they are sow bugs. Sow bugs look like pill bugs, but they cannot roll up.

Pill bug

Sow bug

There is something interesting about sow bugs and pill bugs. They have gills. That may seem strange for animals that live on land. But their gills will not work if they dry out. So these animals must live where it is moist.

Safety Note: *Vacant lots may have sharp or rusty objects. So be careful about where you walk and what you pick up.*

Mouse

Garter snake

Other animals that you might find in a vacant lot are beetles, worms, and snakes. Most snakes are harmless. Still it is better to leave them alone. Then they can eat *pests* such as insects and mice.

Most animals in vacant lots are harmless. But a few are not. If you see scorpions, rats, or black widow spiders, watch, but don't touch.

Sometimes objects in a vacant lot catch and hold rainwater. Old tires, for example, often have little pools in them. Mosquitoes lay eggs in these pools, and the larvae grow up there. Collect some of these larvae in a jar of rainwater. Cover it with a cloth. Then you can watch how the larvae become adult mosquitoes.

Hands off!

Black widow spider

Rat

Scorpion

Looking at plants in a vacant lot. Many kinds of plants grow in a vacant lot. Where there is little grass, the soil often dries out. So only plants with long roots can grow there. The long roots go deep into the soil where there is water.

One kind of a plant with a long root is burdock. Try to dig out a whole burdock root. How deep does it go? What other plants can you find that have roots like this?

Sometimes animals live inside plants. You may be able to find some in burdock. Pick apart several burs until you find some seeds that stick together. With your fingernails pull these apart. Inside you may find a tiny insect larva. This insect gets food and protection from burdock.

Keep a record of the different plants and animals that you find in a vacant lot. Compare this record with the list you made from the lawn sample. In which place—lawn or vacant lot—did you find more? What reasons can you give for what you found out?

OUR SCIENCE HERITAGE

Saving plant communities. John Muir was born almost 150 years ago in Scotland. His family moved to the United States when he was a child. Muir became interested in plant communities. When he grew up, Muir lived in the western United States. He camped and hiked in the mountains and valleys. He wrote about all the special plant communities that he saw.

John Muir wanted to protect the forests, rivers, lakes, and mountains. He wrote to people in Washington, D.C., which helped set up Yosemite and Sequoia as national parks.

President Theodore Roosevelt went on a camping trip with John Muir. Muir showed him the beauty of the wilderness. Later, Mr. Roosevelt set up national parks all over the country to protect the land.

John Muir was an explorer and a *naturalist*. A naturalist is a person who studies nature. He was not the kind of scientist who works in a lab. Muir did his work in the fields and forests. Today, people can enjoy the natural beauty of the land because of John Muir's work to save it.

A Seashore Community LESSON 6

Have you ever visited a seashore? How was it different from a pond or lake? Did the water taste salty? Did you see any big waves? Did the water come up higher on the beach while you were there? Or, did it get lower?

Tides. For several hours the sea water slowly rises. When this happens, people say, "The *tide* is coming in." Then for several hours the water gets lower. People say, "The tide is going out." The sea rises and falls like this about twice a day.

Tide out—tied down! When the tide is high sea water covers much of the beach. Plants such as rockweed float. Small animals swim in and out among the plants looking for food. Crabs and other shellfish search for food, too. Some animals eat, and some animals are eaten.

When the tide is low, pools of sea water may be left behind in the rocks. Animals trapped in the tide pools have to stay there until the tide comes in again. The animals in the tide pools are "tied down." Around the tide pools, rockweed hangs wet and limp. Animals that need to stay wet hide in the rockweed. They hide from the drying sun and from birds that might want to eat them. They wait for the tide to come in.

33

Ideas for REVIEW

■ Almost all soil is a mixture of bits of rock, bits of decayed animal or plant matter and water.

■ Animals take in oxygen and give off carbon dioxide.

■ Plants take in oxygen and give off carbon dioxide too. They also take in carbon dioxide and give off oxygen when making food. Plants usually give off more oxygen than they take in.

■ The plants and animals that live together and interact in a certain place form a community.

■ An animal's color often protects it from its enemies.

■ A desert community has little water. The plants and animals there are adapted to dryness.

■ Most pond animals are adapted to getting oxygen dissolved in water; they are "fenced in" a watery environment.

■ In a vacant lot community, many animals find moist places to live under stones and pieces of junk.

■ At a seashore community, the sea rises and falls about twice a day causing tides.

TEST Your Understanding

On a piece of paper, write the best answer to each of the following questions. *Do not write in this book*.

1. Plants, animals, and weather help a log to
   a. interact
   b. decay
   c. depend
   d. hatch

2. Animals use oxygen that comes mostly from
   a. decay
   b. seeds
   c. green plants
   d. bits of rock

3. Green plants get most of their energy from
   a. sunlight
   b. moonlight
   c. carbon dioxide
   d. oxygen

4. Which of these animals would you probably *not* find in a desert?

   a.
   Tortoise

   c.
   Lizard

   b.
   Spider

   d.
   Frog

5. Where are most desert animals found in the daytime?

6. Many water animals get oxygen through their
   a. fins
   b. shells
   c. mouths
   d. gills

7. Which of these animals cannot get oxygen from water?

   a.
   Fish

   c.
   Clam

   b.
   Crayfish

   d.
   Turtle

8. Which of these animals gets oxygen through gills?
   a. spiders
   b. sow bugs
   c. mice
   d. garter snakes

9. Which of these animals is most "fenced in"?

   a.
   Clam

   c.
   Turtle

   b.
   Dragonfly

   d.
   Water snake

PROBLEMS

1. Suppose that these woods were made into a park. The workers who cared for the park wanted to keep it neat and clean. So they picked up all the dead leaves and sticks.

In time, the woods began to change. The trees did not grow well. Why might this have happened? What other living things might be harmed?

2. Some animals are members of a pond community, but only at times. At other times, they live in other communities. What are some of these animals? List as many as you can think of.

3. This chart lists some birds and what they eat. It tells something about their food and nests. Do you think any could get along in a city community? In a seashore community? Do you think any could live in a desert community? Where else might they live? What reasons can you give?

NAME OF BIRD		WHAT IT EATS	WHAT ITS NEST IS MADE OF	WHERE ITS NEST IS MADE
house sparrow		seeds, insects, garbage, and stuff	grass, cloth, paper, string	holes, cracks, under roofs, almost anywhere
robin		worms, berries	mud and grass	trees or on ledges of buildings
goldfinch		seeds	grass and thistledown	bushes or low trees
song sparrow		seeds, insects	grass	bushes or low in evergreens
mockingbird		berries, insects	twigs and grass	thick bushes

FIND OUT on Your Own

To what kind of community do you belong? What kinds of animals and plants do you interact with most? Using pictures, make a chart of the most important members of your community.

2 Measurement—A Science Process

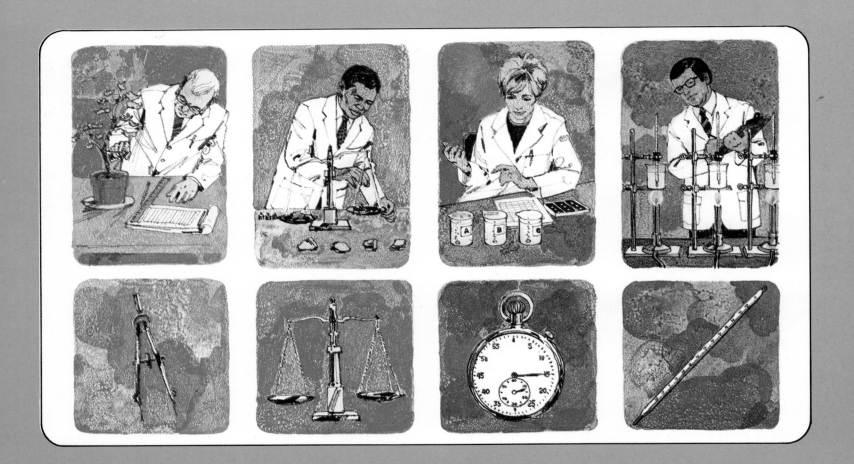

Measurement is an important skill, or *process,* in science. Without measurement, scientists could not record, compare, or describe what they find.

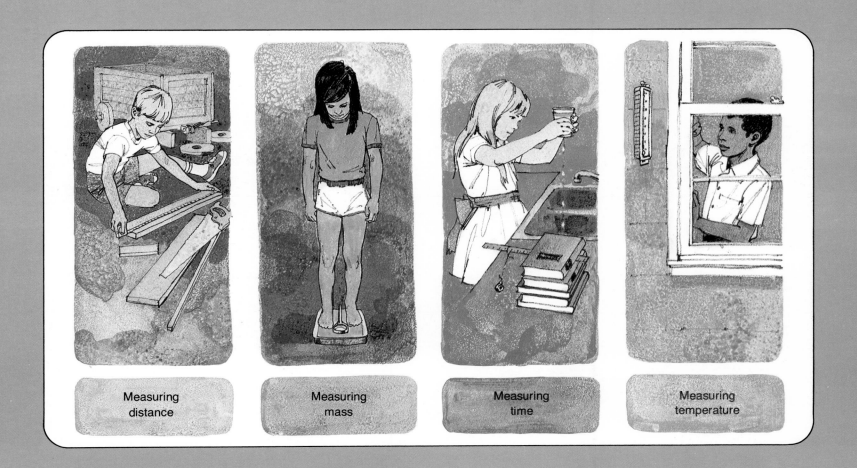

Measuring distance

Measuring mass

Measuring time

Measuring temperature

There are ways to measure distance, mass, time, and temperature. You can use these ways. You can learn to measure things around you.

The marks on these tell how long or how far.

The marks on these tell how hot or how cold.

The marks on these tell how heavy.

The marks on these tell how long or when.

What do these marks tell?

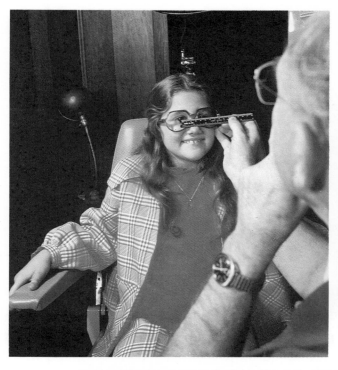

JOBS Using Science

The people in these pictures are measuring distance. They are measuring with a *standard*. They are using standard rulers or tapes. The marks on standard rulers or tapes are the same distance apart as the marks on other standard rulers or tapes.

What are some jobs where it is important to use standard units of distance? What would people working at these jobs measure?

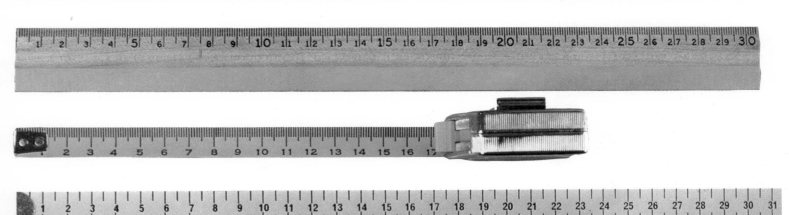

Measuring distance with rulers.

Measuring distance with rulers. Look again at the marks on your ruler. They are part of the *scale*. Each mark on the scale has a number by it. These numbers help you use your ruler to measure. Is the scale on your ruler the same as on other rulers in your room?

Find the place where your scale begins. This is called the zero mark. It is written "0." It is from this point that you should measure. Is it even with the end of your ruler? Or does it start a little way from the end?

One of the measuring tapes has a ring at the end. From what point should you start to measure with this tape?

To measure an object, hold the "0" mark even with the edge of the object. Use a finger to help.

Suppose the "0" mark is not at the end of the ruler. How would you hold the ruler to measure?

SOMETHING TO TRY

1. Use your ruler and a piece of paper.

Draw a line across the paper like this.

Now measure the width of your book. What is

the distance? Mark the same distance on the line you drew.

Measure the length of your book. What is this

distance? Mark it on the same line.

What is the difference between the length and width

of your book?

2. Use your ruler and a piece of string.

With your left hand, hold one end of the string at the

tip of your nose. Hold the other end in your right hand.

Look straight ahead and stretch the string like this.

Now carefully measure the distance the string is stretched.

Record this length with your name on a class chart.

What is the difference between the shortest and the

longest lines on the chart?

Units Used to Measure Distance

LESSON 2

OUR SCIENCE HERITAGE

Measuring with everyday things. The marks on your ruler show the *units* for measuring length. Long ago, there were no rulers with standard units. People used everyday things as units of measurement.

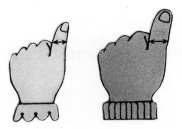

Barleycorns were once used as small units. Not all barleycorns are the same size. The joint of a person's thumb was once used as a small unit. Not all thumb joints are the same size. Were barleycorns and thumb joints good units to use?

The distance from your nose to your fingers was once used as a larger unit. How far is it from your nose to your fingers? How far is it from your teacher's nose to your teacher's fingers? Was this a good unit to use? Why?

People needed a unit of measure that was always the same. They needed a standard unit. A standard was made and kept in a safe place. After that, all rulers were made with units that matched the standard.

Today there are many kinds of rulers. All of them have units based upon the known standard.

The metre. Most people in the world use the *metre* as a distance unit.

The symbol m is used for metre.

1 metre = 1 m

It is about a metre from the floor to

- a door knob.

- a stove top.

- the top of a seat on a school bus.

Is it more or less than a metre

- from the floor to a light switch?

- from the bottom of a chalkboard to the top?

- from the left edge of the door to the right?

- around the top of the wastebasket?

- from the ground to the opening in a mailbox?

45

The centimetre. Look at the ruler below. The distance between the lines is a *centimetre*.

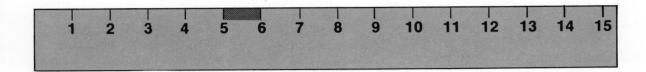

The symbol cm is used for centimetre.

1 centimetre = 1 cm

There are 100 cm in a metre. How many centimetres are on the ruler above?

SOMETHING TO THINK ABOUT

If you have a ruler marked with centimetres handy, you will find that lots of things are about 1 cm long or wide. Take your ruler and measure your sweater buttons. Measure the metal part of your pencil. Measure how long a staple is. Make a list of the things around your classroom that are about 1 cm long or wide.

1. Pin one end of a straw to the center of a big piece of cardboard.

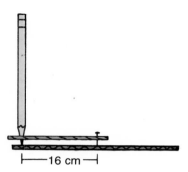

—16 cm—

2. Mark a point on the straw 16 cm from the pin. Push a pencil point through the straw at this mark.

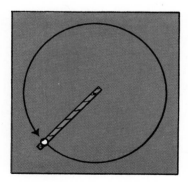

3. Draw a circle with the straw and pencil. Remove the pin, straw, and pencil and cut out the circle.

4. Cut two strips of cardboard 3 cm by 50 cm. Make a hole in one end of each strip. Place one strip on each side of the circle. Use a brass fastener to attach the strips to the center of the circle. Tape this handle as shown.

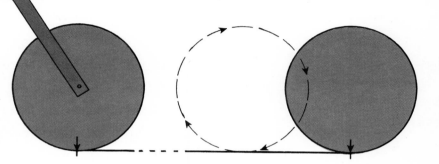

5. Make a mark on the edge of your circle. Where this mark meets the floor draw a chalk line.

Slowly push the circle like a wheel until the mark meets the floor again. Draw another chalk line.

6. Measure the distance between the two chalk lines. It should be about 1 m.

Take your wheel outdoors where there is a straight sidewalk or a large flat playground. Mark off a distance of 100 m. How many turns of your wheel is this?

The world record for running this distance is about 10 seconds. How quickly can you run 100 m?

The millimetre. Look at the ruler on the left. The small unit between each centimetre is called a *millimetre*. There are 10 millimetres in a centimetre. The symbol for millimetre is mm.

10 mm = 1 cm

A dime is about 1 mm thick.

A brand new eraser on the end of a pencil is about 5 mm long.

The boy on the right is holding a metre stick. There are 100 cm in a metre. There are 1000 mm in a metre.

Millimetres are handy whenever you need to measure small things. If you were asked to find out how long a caterpillar's legs are, you could use millimetres. If you were measuring a caterpillar's body, what could you use? If you were measuring how far a caterpillar walks in one day, what could you use?

Can you think of other tiny things you could measure using millimetres?

The kilometre. Millimetres, centimetres, and metres are used to measure short distances. To measure long distances, the *kilometre* is used. *Kilo* means 1000.

A kilometre equals 1000 m. A kilometre is about 11 football fields long.

The symbol km is used for kilometre.

1 kilometre = 1 km

1 km away. You'd have to lay 1000 metre sticks end-to-end to measure 1 km. That is a lot of metre sticks, but a kilometre isn't so long as it sounds.

Look at a map of your neighborhood. What is within 1 km of your school? Is there a library? Is there a park? Are there any offices or stores? If you wanted to walk 1 km, about how many blocks would you need to go? Lots of things are going on within 1 km of where you sit.

How Well Can You Measure? LESSON 3

Which unit to use?

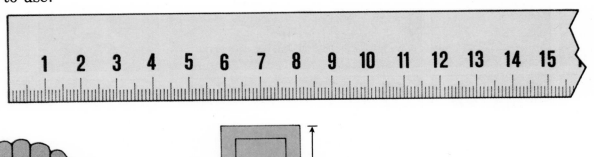

 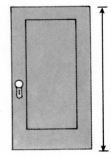 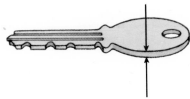

Would you use millimetres, centimetres, or metres to measure these distances?

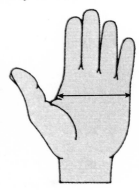 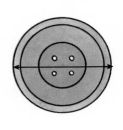 

When people measure these things, what units do they use?

SOMETHING TO TRY

Use a tape measure. Work with a partner.

Record your measurements on a card like this.

Date: _____		Date: _____	
1. height _____	cm	_____	cm
2. head size _____	cm	_____	cm
3. chest (full) _____	cm	_____	cm
4. chest ("empty") _____	cm	_____	cm
5. waist _____	cm	_____	cm

How do you think you will change in three months? In a few months, measure yourself again. How did your body really change? Could you have found out without measuring?

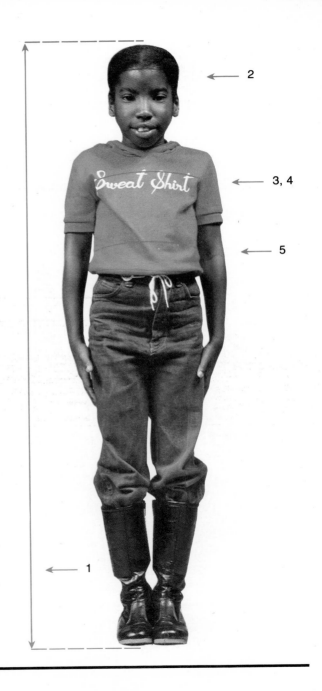

How accurate? Sometimes people need to make *accurate* measurements. They must measure very carefully. Even a 1 mm error would be too much.

Suppose the hole is 1 mm too small. Then the bolt will not go in. Suppose the hole is 1 mm too large. Then the bolt will be loose. Some holes need to be just right. They need to be accurate.

Parts of a watch or a camera need to be measured accurately. They cannot be even 1 mm too large! Or too small! What are some other things that need to be measured accurately?

Some things do not need to be measured accurately. For example, you may wear a belt *approximately* 60 cm long. It doesn't need to be measured accurately. A centimetre too long, or too short, won't matter.

Describe a measurement of distance that must be made accurately. Describe another that can be made approximately.

SOMETHING TO THINK ABOUT

Measurement is important in each of these pictures. Think about which measurements should be made accurately. Which should be made approximately? Which should be most accurate? Which can be the least accurate?

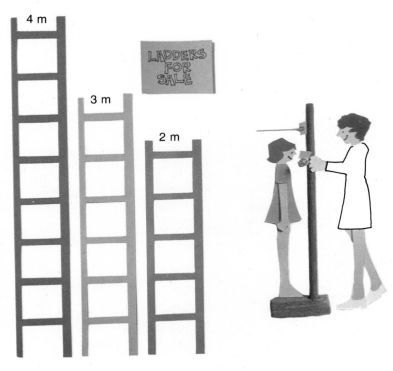

Estimating measurements. Sometimes measurements do not need to be made at all. They can be *estimated*. That means you can make a careful guess of the size of something without using a ruler. Suppose you want to make a jump rope. Could you estimate how much rope to buy? Would you need 4 m of rope? Would 1 m be enough? You probably would estimate about 2 m or a little less. You wouldn't really need to measure. What are some distances that people estimate?

Try estimating the distances across your classroom. Write down your estimates. Then measure, approximately, to see how close you came.

Units Used to Measure Mass   LESSON 4

Mass is the amount of matter in something. This boy is measuring the mass of a duck. What kinds of standard units will he use?

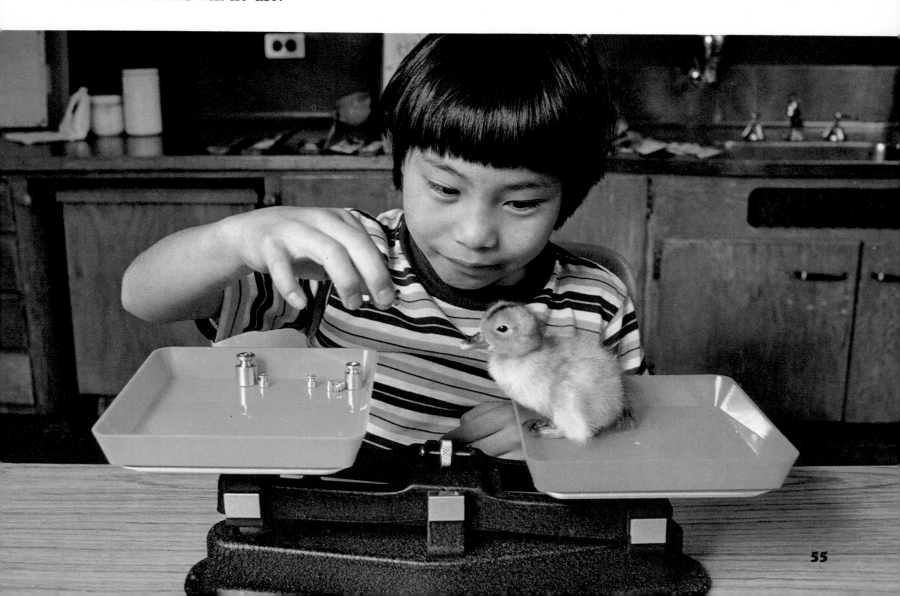

The kilogram. The standard unit of mass is the *kilogram*.

The symbol kg is used for kilogram.

1 kilogram = 1 kg

The empty container shown below is 10 cm long on each side.

10 cm

←10 cm→

When the container is filled with water, the water has a mass of 1 kg. The water in the container *balances* a 1-kg mass. If two things balance each other, they have the same mass.

Twelve flashlight cells balance a 1-kg mass.

How much space? The boy in the picture has measured the masses of different things. He finds that a kilogram of one thing may take up more space than a kilogram of something else. For example, a kilogram of cotton balls takes up lots of space. A kilogram of rocks that are about the same size as cotton balls takes up less space. The rocks have more mass. It doesn't take very many rocks to equal 1 kg. It takes many cotton balls to equal 1 kg.

Apricots have more mass than Ping-Pong balls. Will 1 kg of Ping-Pong balls take up more space than 1 kg of apricots?

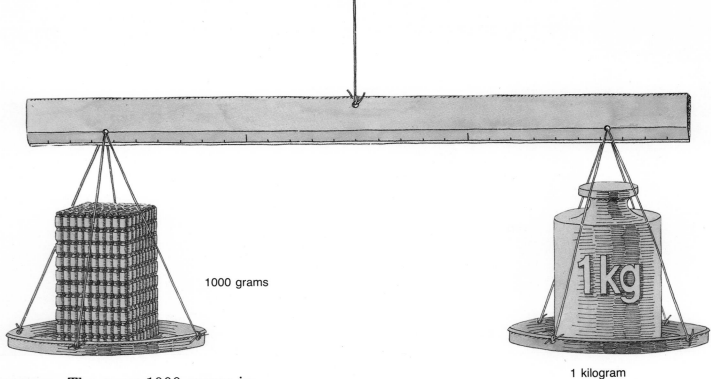

1000 grams

1 kilogram

The gram. There are 1000 *grams* in 1 kilogram.

The symbol g is used for gram.

1 gram = 1 g

A green pea has a mass of about 1 g.

Two paper clips together have a mass of about 1 g.

A nickel has a mass of about 5 g.

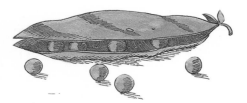

Collect some common small objects. Then find the mass of each in grams. What are some objects that have a mass of about 1 g? 2 g? 5 g? 10 g? 100 g?

Suppose an object has a mass of less than 1 g. Find out how many of these objects it takes to equal 1 g. Make a chart like this.

Objects	How many in 1 g ?
thumbtacks	
pins	
toothpicks	
staples	

Scales and Balances

SOMETHING TO TRY

A *spring scale* measures the pull of *gravity* on an object. The greater the pull of gravity, the more the spring stretches. Rubber bands also stretch.

Use rubber bands to make your own scale like the one shown.

Use any small common objects as standards, such as large nails or large bolts. Put one of your standards in the cup. Mark where the top of the cup comes. That is how far the pull of gravity stretches the rubber bands. Then add more standards, one at a time. Each time you add a standard to the cup, mark where it comes.

Now put in an object. How far down is the cup pulled? How many standards would be pulled the same distance? How heavy is the object in standard units? How can you tell?

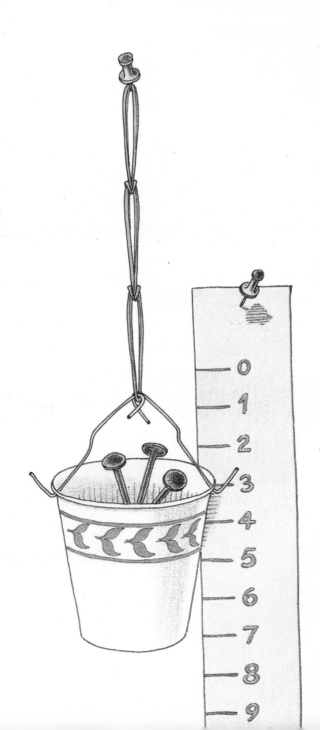

SCIENCE PROJECT IDEA:
MAKING YOUR OWN ROLL-A-MATIC BALANCE

You will need

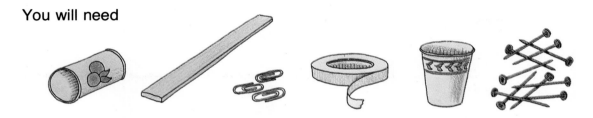

Follow these steps.

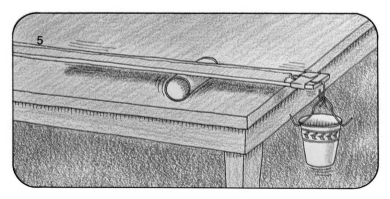

Put a piece of tape along the top of the stick.

Lay the stick across a small can near the edge of a table.

Move the stick back and forth until it almost balances on the can.

Roll the can a *tiny* bit until the stick is level.

Now you are ready to *calibrate,* or put a scale on, your balance.

When the stick is balanced, hold the can still with one hand. With the other, put a mark on the tape right above the balance point. Label this "0," meaning that there are no nails in the cup.

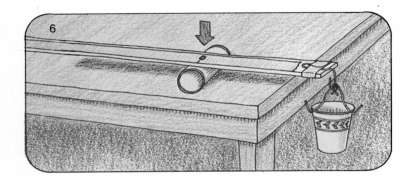

Put one nail in the cup. Move the stick and roll the can until the stick balances again. Then, hold the can and stick still. Put a mark over the balance point.

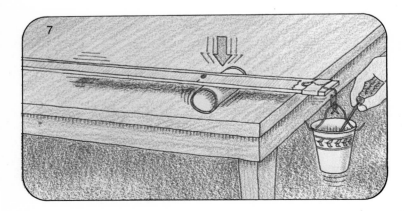

Label it "1."

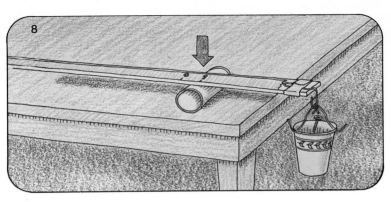

Do this for 2 nails, 3 nails—up to 10 nails. Each time balance the stick and make a mark on the balance point.

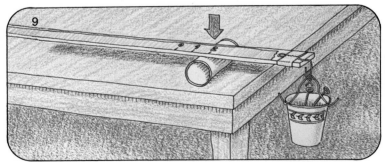

When all the marks are in place, your balance is calibrated. Now find the masses of some small objects in your classroom. Put an object in the cup. Then move the stick and can until the stick balances. What is the mass in "nail units"?

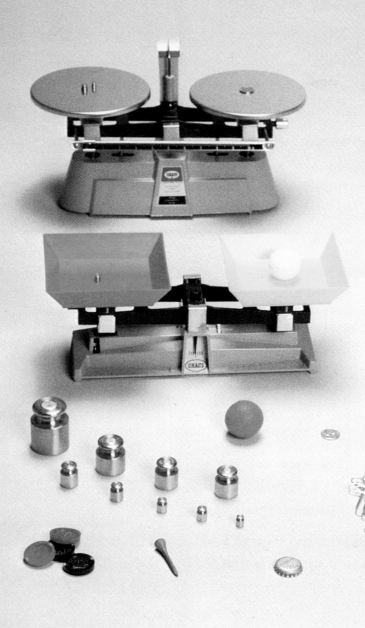

SOME THINGS TO THINK ABOUT

You can find the mass of an object by comparing it with a standard mass. This can be done on a balance. Equal masses balance each other.

Compare the masses of objects like these and give your answers in metric units.

1. What is the mass of a nickel? Do all nickels have the same mass? Would a nickel make a good standard unit? Would a penny make a good standard unit?

2. What is the mass of a table tennis ball? Would it make a good standard?

3. What is the mass of a paper clip? Would it make a good standard?

4. How many paper clips would it take to have a mass equal to a nickel? A penny? A quarter? A table tennis ball?

Ideas for REVIEW

- Measurement is an important skill, or process, in science.

- Measurements are useful when based on a standard used by all people.

- The metre is a world-wide standard unit of length; a doorknob is about 1 m above the floor.

- There are 100 cm in a metre; a thumbtack is about 1 cm across.

- There are 1000 mm in a metre; a dime is about 1 mm thick.

- Long distances are measured in kilometres; 1 km is longer than several city blocks.

- Some measurements must be made accurately; others may be approximated or estimated.

- Mass is the amount of matter in something.

- The kilogram is a world-wide standard unit of mass; 12 flashlight cells have a mass of about 1 kg; so does a pair of men's shoes.

- There are 1000 g in a kilogram; two paper clips have a mass of about 1 g.

- Equal masses balance each other.

TEST Your Understanding

On a piece of paper, write the word or words that make each sentence correct. *Do not write in this book.*

1. The units that have numbers on them are called ____ .

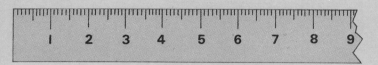

2. When a unit of measurement is the same all over the world, it is called a ____ unit.

3. A dime has a mass of (5 g, less than 5 g, more than 5 g).

4. A spring scale measures the pull of ____ on an object.

5. What is this person doing when she measures a tree this way?
   a. measuring accurately
   b. measuring approximately
   c. estimating

6. Which of these, "a," "b," or "c," is about a metre?

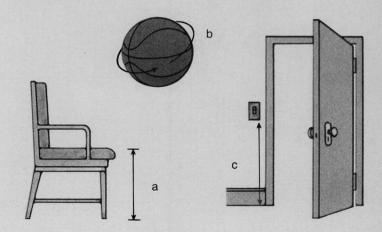

PROBLEMS

1. Measuring length. This person is trying to find the length of a bat. But he has forgotten to do something. What should he do to make the measurement accurate?

2. A banana riddle. When you buy a banana, you pay for the whole mass. But not all the banana is edible. The skin is waste. Suppose that one banana costs 20¢. The whole banana, even when cut into parts, balanced 20 nail units. The skin balanced 10 nail units. Of the 20¢ for the banana, how much is thrown away in skin?

FIND OUT on Your Own

1. Suppose that the threads on a bolt were 1 mm apart. How far would the nut move if the bolt was turned 10 times?

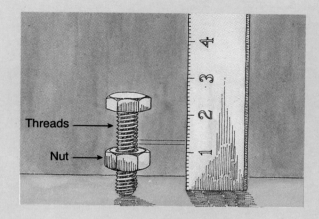

2. Which of these sports objects should have a standard size? Why do you think they should be standard? Which one would vary most in size?

3. A pace is the length of a step when walking on level ground. How do you think your pace would change when

- walking uphill?
- walking downhill?
- running on level ground?

4. Suppose you want a spring balance to be more sensitive. That means it will stretch a lot when only a little mass is added. Should you use

- a chain of a few rubber bands?
- a chain of many rubber bands? Why?

3 Motion and Location

How do you tell when something is moving?

In these pictures, what seems to be moving? How can you tell?

A man is watching the boat. Does he seem to be moving? How can you tell?

Make believe that you are the observer here.
What is moving—the trees, the man, or the sun?

Are you moving? How can you tell?

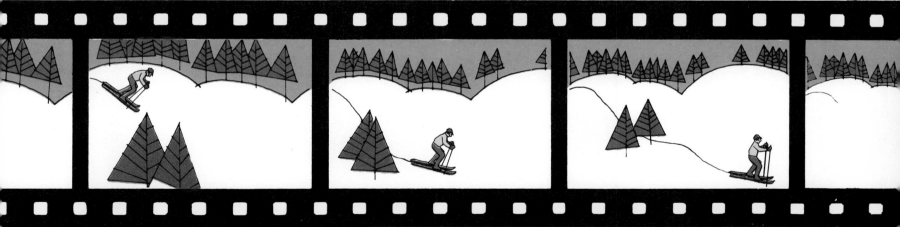

Now make believe you are the observer here. Is
the man moving? Are the trees moving?

Are you moving? How do you know?

69

Things That Move

SOMETHING TO TRY

You can play this game with some friends. Place 10 objects on a table. Have all the players observe where you place each one.

Ask one person to be "it." Have this player turn around and close his or her eyes. Then ask another person to move one of the objects.

Now tell the first player to look at the objects and point to the one that has been moved.

If the first player is right, he or she should choose another player to be "it." Have the first player move another object on the next play. If the first player is wrong, she or he gets another chance.

SOME THINGS TO THINK ABOUT

How can the boy tell that he is in *motion*?

If it were a very dark night, could he still tell?

How can the girl tell that she is in motion? Could she still tell if she closed her eyes?

When your eyes are closed, how can you tell whether you are in motion?

Clues about motion. In the top picture, the woman's boat is anchored so it won't move. The boy on the beach can see that the boat, rocks, and branch are not moving. The streaks behind the boat are a clue that the water is moving.

If the woman just looks at the water, she can't tell whether she is moving or not. Why will looking at the boy make it easy for her to tell that she is not moving? Why will it be hard for her to tell if her eyes are closed?

It is easier to tell what is moving when you can compare it to something standing still. Usually you have enough clues to help you. Sometimes, though, motion can be tricky.

Pretend you are in one of the buses in the bottom picture. One bus moves. Will you be able to tell right away which one it is? What clues will you need?

Look at the girl standing outside the buses. How can she tell which bus moves and which doesn't? How can she tell when both buses move at the same time?

Direction of Motion

Can you tell whether this ball is moving? If it is moving, can you tell which way? Do you need some clues?

Now can you tell whether the ball is moving? Can you tell which way it is moving? What clues did you use?

Can you tell in which *direction* the leaves are moving?

Now can you tell? What clues did you use?

All the children in the picture are in motion.

Which direction
is the girl moving?

Is the girl
moving up or down?

Is the boy
moving up or down?

What clues did you use?

The picture on this page was taken at night. It shows the red tail lights of cars moving down a one-way street. You can see that the cars are moving away from you.

How can you tell that some cars turned right?
How can you tell that some cars turned left?
How can you tell that some went straight?

Kinds of Motion LESSON 3

In these pictures, the objects in color are moving. Which of these objects are moving from one place to another?

Which colored objects are not moving from place to place, but are turning? Which are moving from place to place and also are turning?

What kinds of motion may the colored object at the right have?

How many different kinds of motion does a
merry-go-round have?

SOMETHING TO TRY

1 Throw a ball straight up, and catch it.

What does the motion of the ball look like to you?

What does its motion look like to an observer?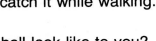

2 Now throw the ball straight up and catch it while walking.

This time what does the motion of the ball look like to you?

What does its motion look like to an observer who is standing still?

What does its motion look like to an observer who is walking with you?

3 Once again throw the ball straight up while walking. But stop walking as soon

as you throw it.

Does the motion of the ball look the same to you as before?

Does its motion look the same as before to an observer

who is standing still?

Does its motion look the same as before to an observer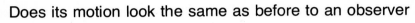

who keeps on walking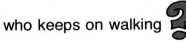

How would you tell someone where the red dot is
on this page?

Turn the page.

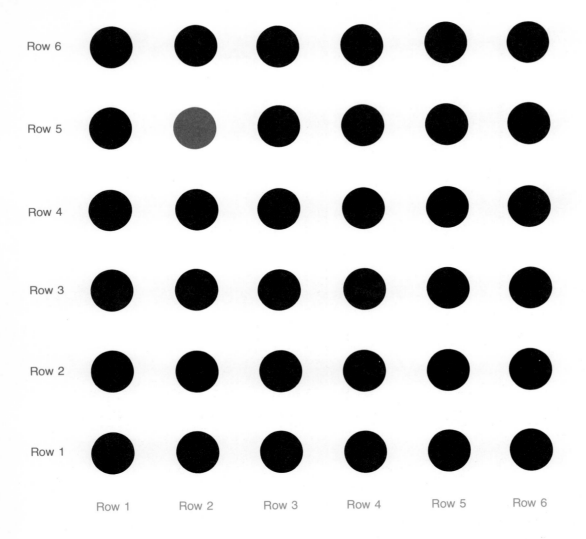

Row 6

Row 5

Row 4

Row 3

Row 2

Row 1

Row 1   Row 2   Row 3   Row 4   Row 5   Row 6

Now is it easier to tell someone the location of the red dot? How would you tell someone where it is? In other words, how would you tell someone its *location?* Why is it easier now to tell someone the location of the red dot?

80

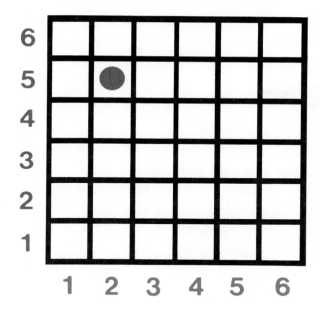

How would you tell someone where the red dot here is?

The lines form a *grid*. Draw a grid like this one on a piece of paper. Number the rows the same way.

Make a dot in one of the squares of your grid. Tell a friend the location of the dot. But do not show your grid to your friend. Ask your friend to make a dot in that location on his or her grid. See whether the dot is in the same location as yours.

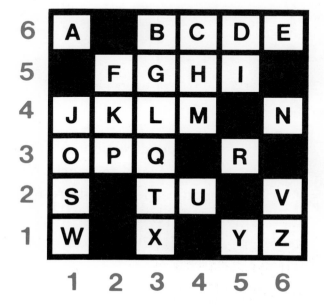

SOME THINGS TO FIGURE OUT

What gets wet as it dries? You can find out with this grid. On a piece of paper, copy the letters at these locations: (3,2), (1,3), (1,1), (6,6), and (3,4).

Using the grid, write your name in numbers.

Using the grid, try to write a secret message.

How many blocks will Ann walk? In what directions will she walk?

How many blocks will Carlo walk? In what directions will he walk?

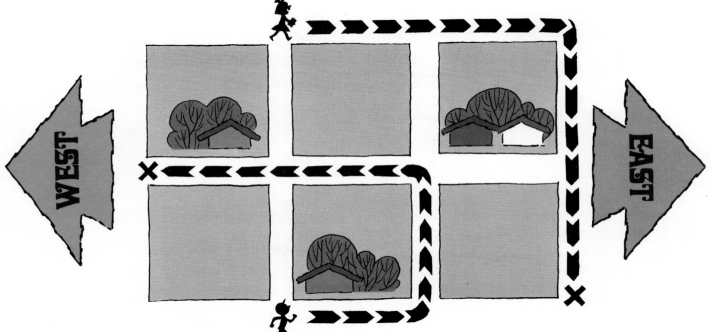

When Carlo and Ann stop, how far will Carlo be from Ann? When they stop, how far will Ann be from Carlo?

In what directions would Carlo have to walk to reach Ann? In what directions would Ann have to walk to reach Carlo?

Using grids. A griddle, or grill, is a metal frame used for cooking. The word grid comes from the word griddle. For centuries, people have found many uses for grids.

In ancient Egypt, artists painted pictures on the walls of tombs. The people and animals in these pictures had to be a certain size. In order to be sure that the sizes were always correct, the artists made a grid on the wall before they drew their pictures. Very important people might be 15 squares tall on the grid. People who were not so important might be only 5 squares tall.

In the 16th century, a man named Mercator used a grid to help him make a map of the world. Grids make it easy to locate certain places on maps and charts. When the streets of cities and towns were first planned, many of them were set up on a grid.

Many different games are played on a grid. Think how hard it would be to play checkers, hopscotch, or football without using a grid!

Ideas for REVIEW

■ As an object moves farther away from you, it looks smaller and smaller.

■ As an object moves closer to you, it looks larger and larger.

■ At times it is hard to tell whether an object is moving.

■ You can tell you are moving when objects not moving seem to move past you.

■ We use certain words to tell someone the direction an object is moving. Some of the words we use are *up, down, right, left, north, south, east,* and *west*.

■ Two kinds of motion are (1) moving from one place to another and (2) turning.

■ If you look at a moving object from different places, its path may look different to you.

■ You can use a grid to locate an object. Maps and many gameboards are grids.

■ You can use distance and direction to tell someone the path of a moving object.

TEST Your Understanding

A. Draw a grid like this one on a piece of paper. *Do not write in this book.* Use the grid to answer questions 1-4.

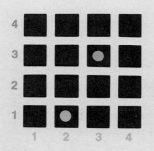

1. What is the location of the red dot?

2. What is the location of the blue dot?

3. On your grid, make an *x* at location 2,2.

4. Make an *r* on your grid at location 1,4.

B. Look at the pictures of the girl in a rowboat. Is she moving toward you or away from you?

C. Use the picture of a girl riding her bicycle to answer questions 5-8.

5. What is the motion of the front wheel?

6. What is the motion of the pedals?

7. What is the motion of the girl's head?

8. What is the motion of the handlebars?

On a piece of paper, write the answer to each question from these choices. The object is

    a. not moving from place to place.

    b. moving from place to place but is not turning.

    c. turning as it moves from place to place.

PROBLEMS

1. Distance and direction

- In drawing this line, how many spaces did the pencil move to the right? Downward? To the left?
- In what other direction did the pencil move? How many spaces did it move in all?
- At which dots did the pencil change its direction of motion? How many times did it change its direction?

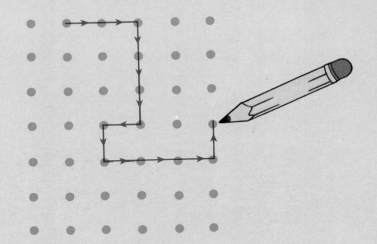

2. Recording motion on a grid

- On a piece of paper, make a dot grid like this one. Be sure to put on it the directions north, south, east, and west.
- Start a dot near the center and draw a line 3 units toward the east. Next draw the line 3 units toward the south. Then draw the line 3 units toward the west and 3 units toward the north.
- What shape did you draw? Is there a change in location between the starting point and the ending point?
- Make another dot grid. Start near the center and draw a line. Draw the line 3 units north, 2 units east, 3 units south, and 2 units west.

- What shape did you draw? Is there a change in location between the starting and ending points?

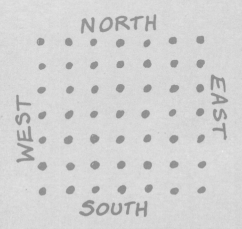

FIND OUT on Your Own

1. You will need a nut tied to a piece of string about 60 cm long. Lie on your back. Ask a friend to swing the nut on the string back and forth about 30 cm above your eyes. What kind of path does the nut seem to follow?

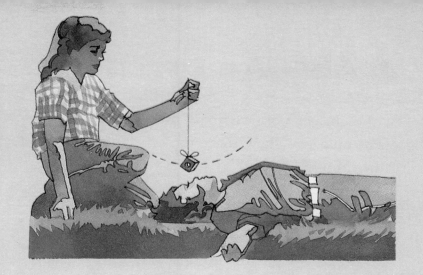

2. You will need a pencil fastened or taped to a record on a turntable. Turn on the record player. Move until your eyes are in line with the pencil. What kind of path does the pencil seem to follow?

3. You will need a road map with letters along one side and numbers along another side. Find out how to use one letter and one number to locate a town on the map.

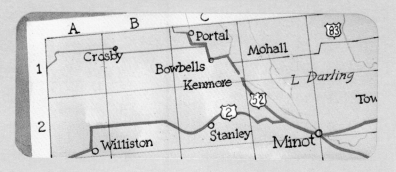

4 Air—An Invisible Push

What can you observe about air?

How could you show there is air around you?

How can air

- bend trees?
- keep you from emptying a wastebasket?
- slow a falling object?
- make waves on a lake?
- hold up a car?
- put bounce in a ball?

Air fills all kinds of spaces.
It fills wastebaskets.
It fills many balls and tires, too.
Can it fill an "empty" room?

Air slows the fall of a parachute jumper.
What would happen if no air were in the way?

Air can slow some objects.
Air can move and lift others.
Air is matter.

Air in the Way LESSON 1

When you roll or squeeze a used plastic bag, it bulges. There must be something inside to cause this. What do you think it is?

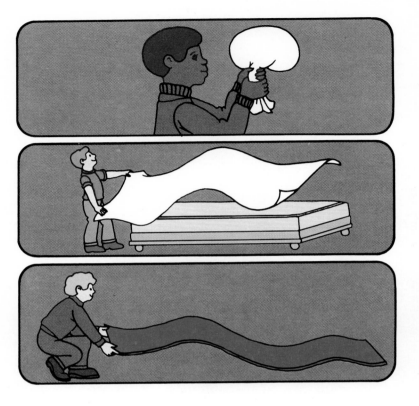

To make a bed, we shake out the sheet. The sheet falls slowly over the bed. What keeps it from falling faster?

You can move a rug more easily if you shake it up and down. What gets under the bulge? What makes you think so?

Air around a door. Suppose you scatter bits of crumpled paper near the crack under a closet door. Then you open the door. What will happen to the paper bits? What causes this?

Now suppose you replace the bits of paper when the door is open. What do you think will happen when you close the door? What does happen?

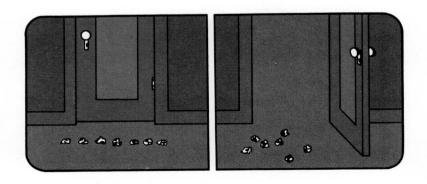

1. Stand at a line. Throw a flat piece of newspaper as far as you can. Measure the distance. How far did it go?

Now, squeeze the paper into a small ball. Throw the paper again.

How far does it go this time? How would you explain the difference?

2. Hold a piece of tagboard like this. Drop it. What sound does it make?

Now, hold the tagboard this way. Drop it again. How does this sound compare with the first sound?

Did the tagboard fall faster the first way or the second way? Explain your answer.

What was between the tagboard and the floor? What happened when the tagboard fell?

3. Make a parachute, using
- a piece cut from a plastic food bag
- tape
- some string
- a ball of clay

Go outdoors to try it out.

What should you do to throw it up high? Why does it come down more slowly than it goes up?

Air Takes Up Space LESSON 2

SOMETHING TO TRY

1. Fill an aquarium so that the water is about 3 or 4 cm from the top. Stuff a sheet of tissue into the bottom of a clear plastic tumbler. Turn the tumbler upside down. Slowly press it down into water. Do you think the water will wet the tissue? Keep pressing the tumbler straight down. What seems to be happening to the tumbler? When you reach the bottom, lift it back out. Feel the tissue. Is it wet or dry? How would you explain what you observed?

2. Put your thumb tightly over the opening of a funnel. Then push the funnel down into a container of water as shown. Ask a partner to mark the water level of the container. Then have him or her hold a hand over your thumb. Remove your thumb. What does your partner feel? What happened to the water level in the container? What happened to the water level in the funnel? How would you explain what you observed?

Remove the funnel. Put your thumb over it again. This time push it down until your thumb is under water. Slowly move your thumb from the top of the funnel. What happens?

Pouring air. Can you pour air from one tumbler into another? You can—if you do it under water. Here's how. First, let one tumbler fill with water. Then turn it upside down and hold it there. Turn the other tumbler upside down and press it down into the water. When its opening is below the first tumbler, tip it slightly. See if you can catch the air bubbles in the first tumbler. Can you catch them all? Try not to "spill" any air!

Now try to pour the air back into the other tumbler. How is pouring air in water different from pouring water in air? What is different?

There is a hole through the funnel but water doesn't run into the bottle. It can't run in unless the air can get out. Water and air cannot take up the same space at the same time. They can only trade places.

Can you think of a way to let the water in? You can test your idea with a funnel, some clay, and a bottle. Does it work? What has to leave the bottle for water to enter?

1. Some bottles and jugs have handles like this. What do you think the purpose of this handle is? How could you test your idea?

2. Suppose you had an "empty" container. Then you filled it with some dry sand. Would all the air come out of the container when you poured in the sand? How could you find out?

3. Suppose you hold an open milk carton upside down. Then you press it down into a container of water. How can you tell whether water comes up into the carton? Can you think of another way?

4. Suppose you had a job as a "jug-emptier." The faster you can empty a jug, the more you get paid. What is the fastest way to empty a jug without breaking it? Test your ideas.

Air Can Push on Things LESSON 3

Pushes in all directions. Suppose you were to hold a large balloon inside an "empty" can. Then suppose you blew down into the balloon until it filled up the can. Could you make the balloon press against the sides of the can? Why do you suppose this happens if you blow down?

Could you lift the can by holding the neck of the balloon tightly closed? How heavy a can could you carry with the help of air?

This girl placed a plastic bag flat on the table. Then she covered it with her book. When she blows into the bag, what will happen?

In which direction does she blow? In which direction does the air push?

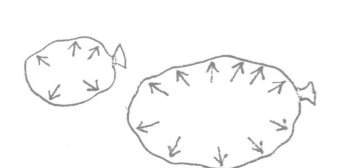

More surface, more push! In a small bag, air cannot press on many places. One small bag by itself cannot hold up a very large object.

In a large bag, air has many places to press. It does not press hard on any one place. But there are many places that it can press. The total of all these presses is large.

95

Bubble buildings. Bubbles have a history as old as the earth. Gum bubbles have a history as old as that of gum. But bubble buildings were first used in 1917. They are recent. One of the first large bubble buildings was the Japanese pavilion at the World Expo in 1970. Today, the roofs of many sports buildings are held up by air. A famous one is the Metrodome in Minneapolis. Its air-supported roof covers a football field.

A famous architect, Buckminster Fuller, dreamed of an air dome over part of New York City. His dream roof would keep out dirt, rain, hail, and snow, but let in sunlight. Such a roof is only a dream now. But walking on the moon was a dream not so long ago.

Dome roofs are held up by slight air *pressure*. The air pressure comes from blowers or fans that run all the time. When someone opens the door to such a building, a little air escapes. But the fans blow more air back into the building. Someday, perhaps you will work or live in a building held up by air.

SOMETHING TO TRY

With 12 to 15 classmates, kneel around a large table. Each of you should have a plastic bag. Lay the bags flat on the table with the openings sticking over the edge.

Some helpers should turn an identical table upside down on top of the bags. Be sure that most of each bag is between the tables.

Your teacher may want to sit on the top table.

Gather the opening, ready to blow into the bag. At a signal from your teacher, everyone should blow. What happens? Are you surprised?

Suppose the tables were so large that everyone in school could have a bag to blow into. How much do you think could be lifted?

Putting Air to Work

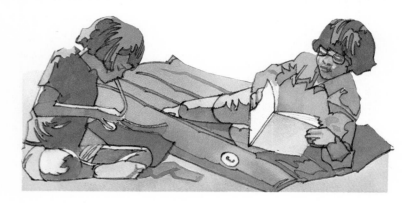

This girl *compresses* the air in an air mattress. Then it can hold her off the ground. How is an air mattress like a tire?

Compressed air. A soft tire needs more air in it. A tire pump squeezes air into a small space. It compresses the air. The compressed air pushes hard in all directions. It pushes on the handle and on the sides of the pump. If you push hard enough, compressed air goes into the tire.

Compressed air in a tire pushes outward. It pushes equally on every place inside the tire. It pushes down as well as up. It pushes down hard enough to hold up the car.

A football has compressed air in it. Kicking it compresses the air even more. Then what happens to the football?

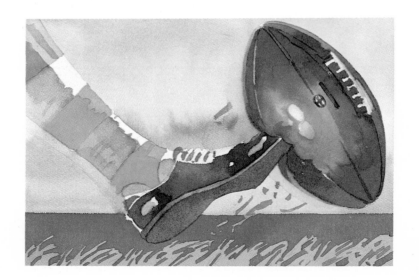

JOBS Using Science

Rita's mother and father operate a service station. Some of their tools work by compressed air. Air is compressed by a motor-driven pump. The compressed air is stored in a strong tank. It is carried by strong hoses to the tools that need it.

An air wrench loosens and tightens nuts.

Compressed air helps send oil and grease to places that need them.

Compressed air lifts the car so that a person can work underneath it.

Perhaps you can visit a service station. Ask the operator to show you how some of the compressed air tools work.

SOMETHING TO TRY

With your teacher's help, you can make this model. It shows how compressed air lifts a car.

Use a mailing tube, a cork, and a straw.

Near one end of the tube, cut a hole so the cork will fit in tightly. Put the cork in place. Make a hole through the cork just big enough for a straw. Put both the straw and cork in place. Put a toy car on top. Blow through the straw. What happens?

Ideas for REVIEW

- Air is matter and takes up space.

- Air can move things, or get in the way of moving things.

- Air tends to fill all spaces not filled with something else.

- Air can be "poured" or moved from one container to another.

- Air gets pushed out of an "empty" container when something else is put in.

- A lot of little pushes can have the same effect as one large push.

- The larger the surface on which air can push, the greater its total push.

- Compressed air presses equally hard in all directions.

- Air under pressure operates many machines and tools.

TEST Your Understanding

A. Choose the picture or words that best answer each question. Write the letter of your answer on a piece of paper. *Do not write in this book.*

1. Which of these can a person do?
   - **a.** carry air
   - **b.** see air
   - **c.** smell air
   - **d.** taste air

2. Which one is impossible to do?
   - **a.** empty a glass
   - **b.** pour air under water
   - **c.** squeeze air
   - **d.** sit on air

3. How would you hold a tumbler of air under water so it doesn't spill?

   a   b   c   d

4. Suppose you fill a balloon with air. Then you squeeze it. The air
   - **a.** presses toward the neck
   - **b.** presses in all directions
   - **c.** presses only down
   - **d.** presses only into the center

5. Which of these holds air under pressure?

   - **a.** empty bottle
   - **c.** slice of bread

   - **b.** soap bubble
   - **d.** eraser

B. On your paper, write answers to each of the following:

6. List five things that use compressed air.

7. Suppose a very large, flat sheet of wood falls over on a smooth floor. What kind of sound would it make? Why?

8. Suppose a car enters a garage. As the car goes in, what happens to the air in the garage? Why?

9. Write two sentences about air. Use as many of these words as you can:

space	compressed	invisible	pressure
matter	work	empty	moves

PROBLEMS

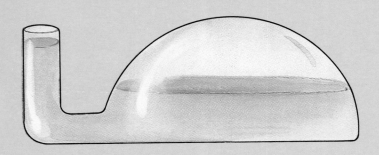

1. Suppose a container looks like this. You want to fill it with water. But when you try it, the water stops going in. What could you do to fill it with water?

3. Suppose you had a huge plastic bag—the world's biggest bag! It is made of the same plastic that you used in class. Could you hold up an elephant? Why?

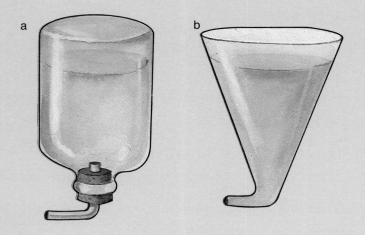

2. Animals in cages need water. Which of these ways to supply water works best? Why?

FIND OUT on Your Own

1. What causes the "Ssss . . ." after a large truck has stopped? How could you find out?

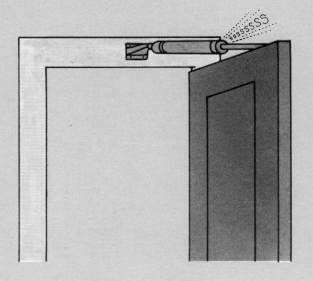

2. What causes the "Ssss . . ." when this door closes?

3. Ask a service station operator for an old tire valve. How does it work? How does air get into the tire? Why can't it get out?

5 Bones and Muscles

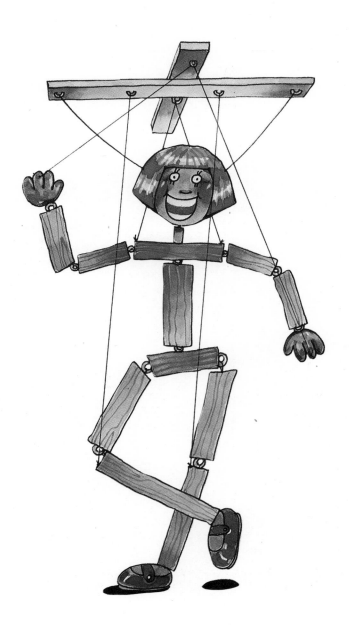

Have you ever seen a stick-and-string puppet?

Have you ever made one move?

Perhaps your class can make some puppets like those shown here.

What helps the puppets to stand up straight?

What makes them move?

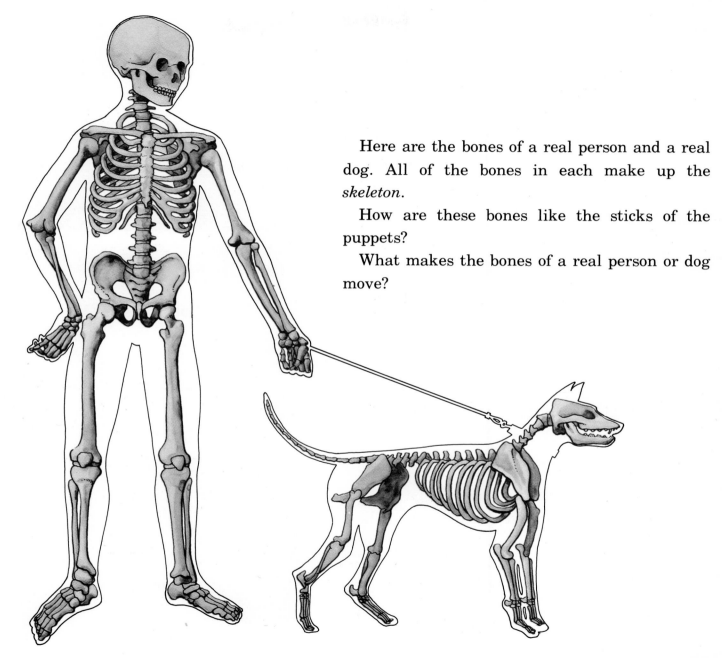

Here are the bones of a real person and a real dog. All of the bones in each make up the *skeleton*.

How are these bones like the sticks of the puppets?

What makes the bones of a real person or dog move?

Bones Protect and Support the Body LESSON 1

The skull. The bones of the head are called the *skull*. The brain is inside the skull. The skull protects the brain.

The skull has 22 bones. Most of them fit together tightly. You cannot tell by feeling that they are separate bones. Try it and see. Which bone of the skull is the only bone that moves?

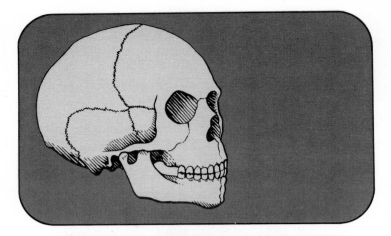

The backbone. You can feel the bones in your neck and down the middle of your back. This chain of bones is called the backbone, or *spine*. The skull rests on the backbone.

There are 33 bones in your backbone. By the time you are grown, some of them will have grown together. Then there will be only 26 bones in your backbone.

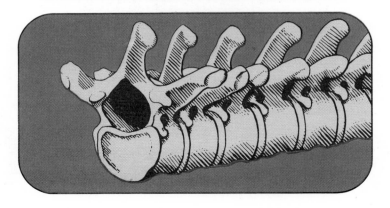

Each bone in your backbone is called a *vertebra*. More than one vertebra are called *vertebrae*. Each vertebra has a hole through its center. The *spinal cord* runs through this hole. The spinal cord carries signals between the brain and other parts of the body. Your backbone protects your spinal cord. Your backbone helps you walk upright.

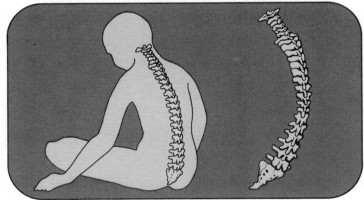

The breastbone and the ribs. In the middle of your chest is a large flat bone. It is called the breastbone. Look at the picture. How many pairs of ribs are attached to the breastbone? What are the ribs attached to in the back?

Two pairs of ribs are called "floating" ribs. Can you guess which pairs they are? Why do you think they are called floating ribs?

The breastbone, ribs, and backbone form a kind of cage. It is called the *rib cage*. The rib cage protects your lungs and heart.

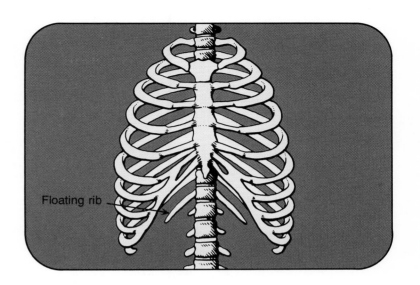

Floating rib

SOMETHING TO TRY

1. Feel your breastbone. Feel where your ribs are attached to your breastbone. Find where your ribs are attached to your backbone.

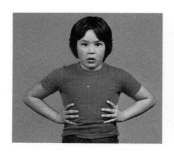 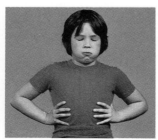

2. Put your hands above your waist as shown in the picture. Can you feel your ribs moving in and out?

3. Make your rib cage get larger or smaller when you take a deep breath. Try it and see.

4. Make your rib cage as small as you can. Ask a classmate to measure the distance around your rib cage with a piece of string. Now make your rib cage as large as you can. Ask your classmate to measure your rib cage again. Using a ruler, find out how much your rib cage has changed.

The hipbones. Put your hands on your waist. Your hands are resting just above your hipbones. Feel your hipbones with your fingers. You have one hipbone on each side. They are two of the largest bones in your body.

What other bones are your hipbones attached to? How you do think hipbones help you walk?

The upper legbones. Look at the drawing on the right of the girl's hipbones and legbones. Each upper leg has one bone. They are the longest and heaviest bones in your body.

The lower legbones. You may be surprised that there are two bones in your lower leg. Feel the bone in the front of your lower leg. It is the one that gets banged on things. It is called the *shinbone*. Put one hand on the inside of your ankle. Put the other on the inside of your knee. Those are the two ends of your shinbone.

The smaller bone in your lower leg is called the *calfbone*. Put one hand on the outside of your ankle. Put the other on the outside of your knee. Those are the two ends of your calfbone.

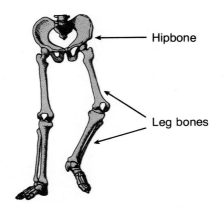

Hipbone

Leg bones

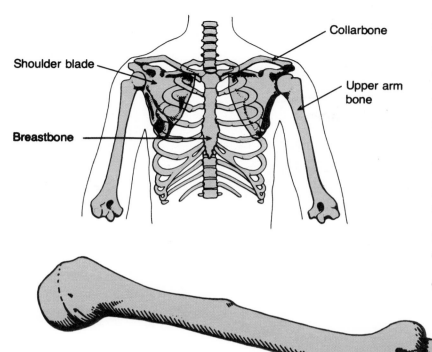

Shoulder blade

Collarbone

Upper arm bone

Breastbone

The collarbones and the shoulder blades. The two long bones near the base of the neck are the *collarbones*. Feel your collarbones. Can you tell where the ends of each of your collarbones are attached?

One end of each collarbone is attached to the breastbone. The other end is attached to the shoulder blade. You have two shoulder blades. They are broad flat bones in your upper back. Try to find them.

The arm bones. The bones in your arms are quite similar to the bones in your legs.

SOMETHING TO TRY

1. Feel the bones in your arms. How many bones are there in your upper arm? How many bones are there in your lower arm?

At one end, the bone in the upper arm is attached to a shoulder blade. At the other end, it is attached to the bones in the lower arm. Feel the other end of each bone at your elbow.

2. At your wrist, feel one end of each bone in your lower arm. Feel the other end of each bone at your elbow.

3. Find a bony bulge at your wrist. Look at the picture and find the bone that has the bulge.

How are your arm bones like your leg bones? How are they different from your leg bones?

Bones and How They Move

Cartilage. Where two bones meet, there is usually a pad of *cartilage*. Cartilage is softer than bone. It is also slippery. Cartilage helps protect bones against damage from bumps.

There is a pad of cartilage between each two vertebrae. The cartilage makes it easier for you to twist and bend your backbone. There is cartilage between the ribs and the breastbone. This makes it possible for your ribs to move in and out when you breathe.

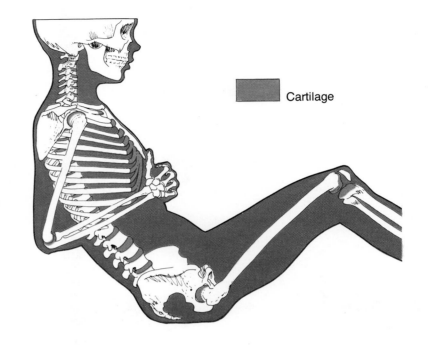

Cartilage

Joints. The place where one bone is joined to another bone is called a *joint*. Your wrist, shoulder, and knee are joints. Can you think of some other joints in your body?

Your knee is like a hinge. It lets you move the lower part of your leg back and forth. But it does not let you swing it from side to side. Your knee is called a *hinge joint*. Where are there other hinge joints in your body?

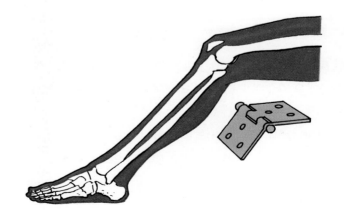

1. Sit on a strong table and let your legs hang down. Then swing the lower part of one leg back and forth. Does the upper part of the leg move as you do this?

Next, swing the lower part of your leg from side to side. Can you keep the upper part still?

Hold one leg straight out in front of you. Try swinging the lower part from side to side without moving the upper part. Can you do it?

2. Hold one arm straight out at the side. Then, without bending your arm, move your hand in a circle. Your shoulder is a *ball and socket* joint. How does it let you move your arm?

3. Now, bend one arm as shown. Move your hand in a circle. Hold on to your upper arm while you do this. What can you feel your upper arm doing?

4. In most hinge joints, such as your knee, both parts can move. Your jaw is also a hinge joint. Use your hands to show how you think your jaws move when you chew.

Now, chew a bit of cracker while your nose rests on your desk. Chew another bit while your chin rests on the desk. Do both jaws move, or does only one move?

JOBS Using Science

Some scientists search for clues to plants and animals that lived long ago. These scientists are called *paleontologists*. Paleontologists are science detectives.

The woman in the picture is a paleontologist. She is studying the bones of a dinosaur that lived long ago.

Just as some animals today have skeletons, so did some animals of long ago. Often the bones of these animals are all that is left of them.

Paleontologists search all over the world for these bones. They also search for other clues. Sometimes they find teeth of animals that lived long ago. Mostly they find only bits of bones.

Sometimes paleontologists guess at the size and shape of bones missing from a skeleton. They may guess at how an animal moved. They also may guess at the kind of food it ate and the place where it lived. What clues do you think they would have?

Muscles and How They Move

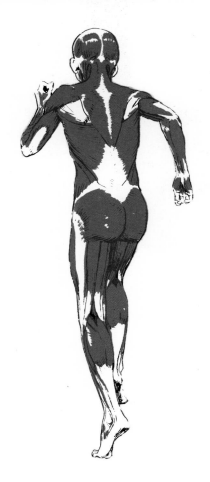

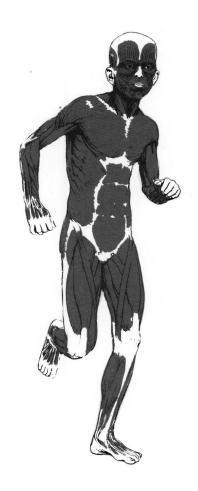

Animals move in special ways. Birds fly or hop, fish swim, and snakes slither. People walk and run. They all use muscles to move.

Suppose you could step out of your skin. What would you look like?

You could see the muscles that give the "pulls" to make you move. Without these muscles, you could not run or throw a ball. You could not even get out of bed in the morning!

Muscle fibers. Muscles and other parts of your body are made up of *cells*. The cells in most muscles are joined together in a certain way. Groups of these cells are called *fibers*. Muscle fibers are something like the fibers in a string.

Muscles are usually attached to bones by sets of tough fibers called *tendons*.

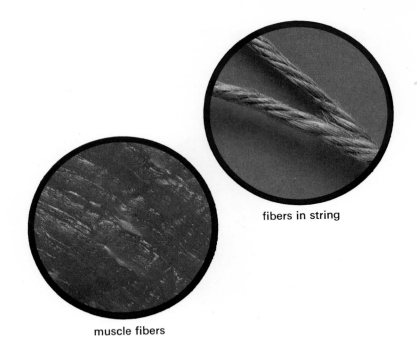

fibers in string

muscle fibers

Muscles and movement. Almost all of the movements you make happen when muscles become shorter, or *contract*. When a muscle contracts, it pulls on the tendons. The tendons then move parts of the body. A muscle between two bones pulls the bones toward each other. Not all of your bones move easily. Some move more easily than others. Some do not move at all.

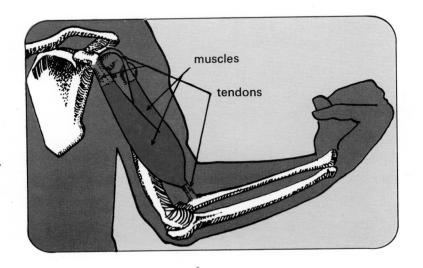

muscles

tendons

114

Hold one hand, palm up, against the bottom of your desk. With your other hand, feel the muscles of your upper arm. As you push up on the desk, feel the muscles again. Which muscle contracts, the front one or the back one?

Lay your hand, palm up, on the top of the desk. As you push down on the desk, feel the muscles of your upper arm. Which muscle contracts? Does your leg work the same way? How could you find out?

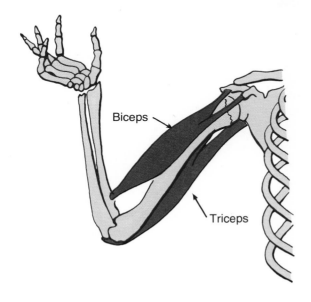

Biceps

Triceps

Pairs of muscles. One muscle pulled your lower arm up. Another muscle pulled it down.

Muscles can only pull. They cannot push. When muscles stop pulling we say they *relax*. The muscle that pulled your lower arm up cannot push it down. Another muscle pulled it down.

115

In the top two drawings, a ruler is taped to a desk. It will move when pulled or pushed. Could you move the ruler by pushing on a string? Of course not! But if you pull on a string, the ruler moves—as long as the other string is loose.

Muscles work in pairs to move bones back and forth. When one muscle of a pair contracts, the other muscle relaxes.

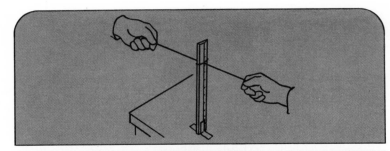
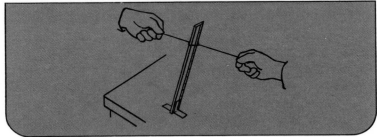

SOMETHING TO TRY

Try to write the letter "E" with a pencil held by eight strings. Ask three classmates to help you. Each person holds two strings as shown.

How must you pull the strings to move the pencil? Is it easy to write this way?

Now, hold the pencil in your hand and write your name. How do your fingers move? Try to find out which muscles pull your fingers.

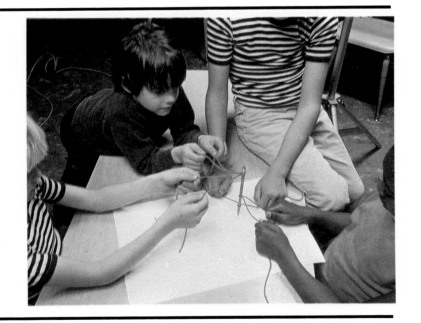

Testing muscle strength. The boy in the top picture is testing to see how strong his legs are. He is pushing as hard as he can against a bathroom scale. The scale measures how hard he can push.

If the boy can't push very hard, he needs to build up his leg muscles. He can spend some time running, bending, jumping, and bicycling. Then he can try again.

The girls in the picture are arm wrestling. The idea is to push the other person's arm down flat on the table. In order to win, it helps to have strong arms. Arm muscles aren't the only ones being used, though. Back, chest, and shoulder muscles are working hard, too.

117

Building muscle pairs. When you walk, play ball, or ride a bicycle, you use many pairs of muscles. Muscles that you often use become larger and stronger.

Regular exercise helps to build stronger muscles. This means exercising for a certain amount of time each day or every other day. Here are some helpful exercises.

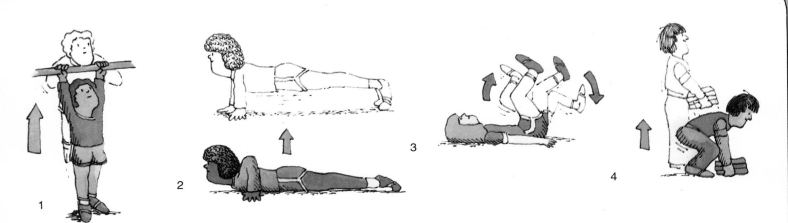

1. Chin-ups help strengthen the front muscles of your upper arms. At first, try only one. As your muscles become stronger, try one more. Increase the number of chin-ups you do one at a time.

2. Try some push-ups. They help strengthen the muscles of your arms and stomach.

3. Lie on your back. Lift your legs a little way off the floor. Then move them as if you were riding a bicycle. Which muscles are you making stronger?

4. You can help many muscles become stronger by lifting things. But the things must not be too heavy. Begin with something you can lift easily. As your muscles grow stronger, lift something a little heavier. **Safety note:** *When you lift something, bend your knees but keep your back straight. Lift things with your legs, not your back.*

Running and swimming are good exercises for your leg, arm, and chest muscles. So are most games and sports.

An exercise tool. Many people exercise by playing ball games. There are over thirty games that can be played with balls.

The very first ball games may have been played with round stones. People may also have used green fruit or coconuts to play ball games. Early settlers in North America made balls out of pigs' stomachs.

Two ball games played today were invented by teachers. They are volleyball and basketball. Find out who invented each of these games.

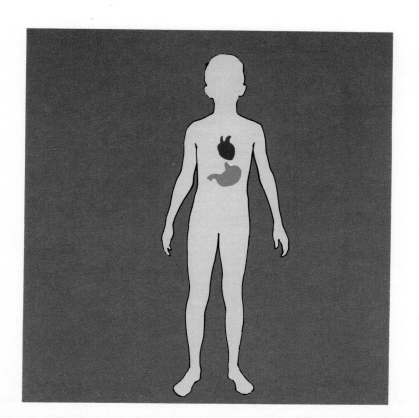

Muscles you cannot control. Many muscles contract and relax only when you want them to. They are called *voluntary* muscles.

Other muscles contract and relax whether you want them to or not. They are called *involuntary* muscles. Your heart muscle is an involuntary muscle. You cannot control it. Whether you are asleep or awake, it is contracting and relaxing. The muscles in your stomach are involuntary, too. They contract and relax when your stomach has food in it. You do not even have to think about them. They work all by themselves.

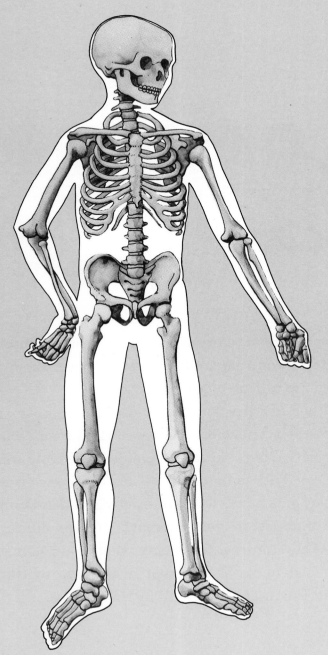

Ideas for REVIEW

■ All the bones in your body make up your skeleton.

■ Bones protect and support the body. For example, your skull protects your brain. Your hipbones support the upper part of your body.

■ There usually is a pad of cartilage where two bones meet. Cartilage helps protect bones against damage from bumps.

■ A joint is the place where one bone is joined to another bone.

■ Paleontologists search for clues to plants and animals that lived long ago.

■ Tendons connect muscles to bones.

■ Muscles work in pairs to move bones back and forth.

■ Muscles can only pull. They cannot push.

■ Regular exercise can help you build strong muscles in most parts of your body.

■ You can control voluntary muscles, such as the muscles in your legs.

■ You cannot control involuntary muscles, such as your heart muscle.

TEST Your Understanding

Use the words from the following list to make each sentence correct. Not all the words are used. Write your answers on a piece of paper. *Do not write in this book.*

tendons   spinal cord
fibers   hinge
lower   breastbone
voluntary   upper
contract   involuntary
vertebra   relaxes
rib cage   skeleton

1. Each bone in your backbone is called a ____ .

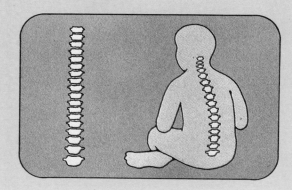

2. Your backbone protects your ____ .

3. The breastbone, ribs, and backbone make up the ____ .

4. One end of a collarbone is attached to a shoulder blade. The other is attached to the ____ .

5. There is one bone in each ____ leg.

6. Your knee is a ____ joint.

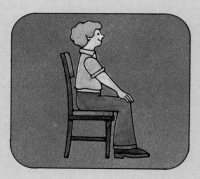

7. Muscles become shorter and thicker when they ____ .

8. When a muscle contracts it pulls on the ____ .

9. When one muscle in a pair contracts, the other one ____ .

10. The muscles in your arms are ____ muscles.

PROBLEMS

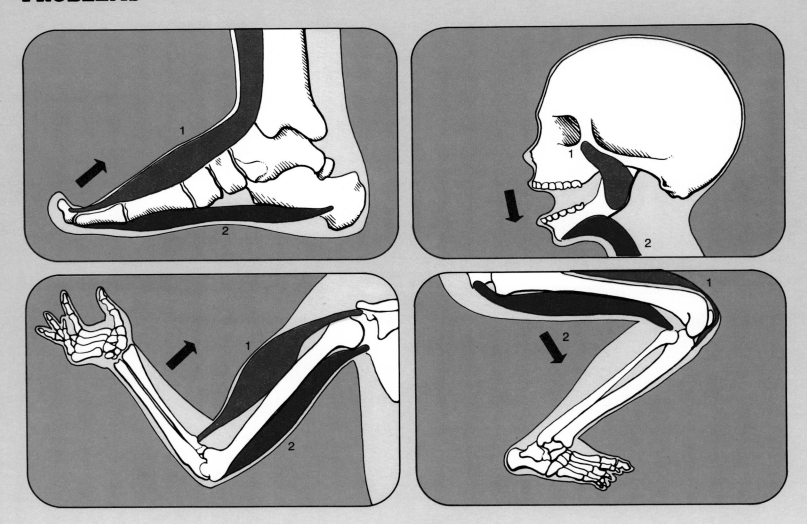

1. In each picture, which muscle is pulling? What would happen if the other muscles shown were pulling instead?

2. Imagine that this make-believe clay animal has two kinds of muscles. There are circular muscles running around the animal. There are lengthwise muscles running from end to end.

Now, suppose that all the lengthwise muscles relaxed and the circular muscles contracted. What would happen to the animal's shape? Suppose the circular muscles relaxed and the lengthwise ones contracted. What would happen?

Many animals with muscles do not have a skeleton. But they can move just the same. Using this model, explain how an earthworm moves.

FIND OUT on Your Own

Find some animal tracks to study. How do you think the animal was moving when it made the tracks? Was it hopping? Was it walking? Was it running or galloping?

How many legs does the animal have? If it has four legs, compare the size of its feet. Are its back feet larger, smaller, or the same size as its front feet? Can it use its front feet like hands? If it has two legs, are its feet like those of a bird?

What kind of animal do you think made the tracks?

Here are the footprints of an animal that draws in its claws when it walks. This helps keep them sharp. What kind of animal makes footprints like these?

Back footprint   Front footprint

Here are the footprints of an animal that can use its front paws like hands. Do you know what animal makes footprints like these?

6 Shadows and Light

Have you ever played "shadow tag"? It is easy and fun to play.

Keep moving so that your friend cannot step on your shadow. When your friend does tag your shadow, it is your turn to be "it."

Could you play shadow tag on a cloudy day?

Could you play shadow tag at night?

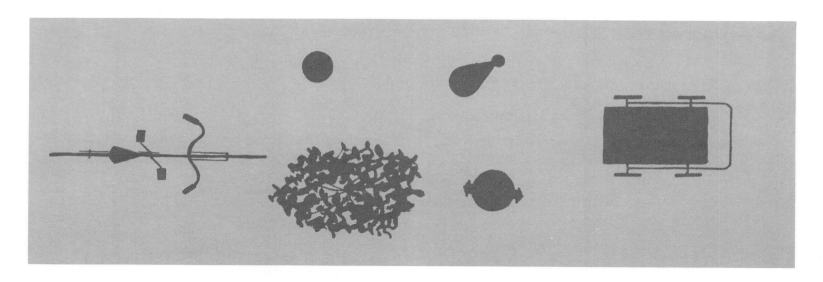

The drawings above and below show the shadows of six things. Can you match them? Can you tell what things made them?

What are shadows? What makes shadows? Why do shadows change?

Shadows and How They Change LESSON 1

These children want to make a shadow. How can they do this?

There is no shadow in this picture. Why not?

At last, there is a shadow.

What two things did the children need to make a shadow? Where did each thing have to be?

Again there is no shadow. Why not?

SOMETHING TO TRY

1. Use your hands to make shadows on a screen or wall. Hold your hands up so they block the bright light.

With your hands, can you make shadows that look like animals?

2. Make shadows using things like blocks and balls. Also try using jar lids and cardboard tubes.

What things were used to make the shadow shapes below?

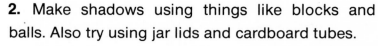

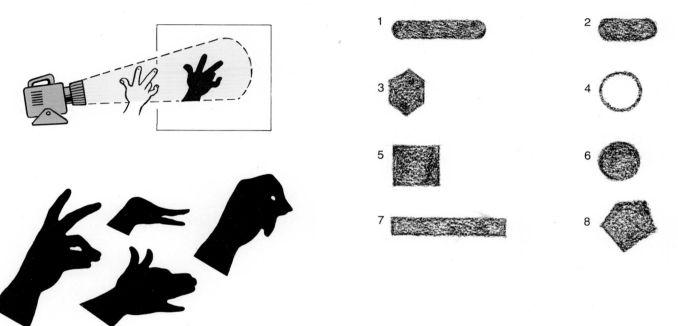

1

2

3

4

5

6

7

8

SOME THINGS TO THINK ABOUT

1. These students are measuring a shadow.

How could they make the shadow longer? How could they make it shorter?

You can try this yourself!

2. Curved objects can *cast* straight shadows. And straight objects can cast curved shadows.

Which of these curved objects can cast straight shadows? How could you tell for sure?

3. How could you make a straight ruler cast a curved shadow? Could you do this without bending the ruler?

Shadow size and sharpness. Look at the pictures. In one the pencil is close to the projector. In the other the pencil is close to the screen. Predict which pencil will cast the larger shadow.

Now test your prediction. Hold two pencils at the same distance from a screen. Then move one toward the screen. Move the other toward a light. Which shadow gets larger? Which gets sharper?

Can a shadow get larger and sharper at the same time?

Can a shadow get smaller and fuzzier at the same time?

You can make a shadow sharper by moving the object toward the screen.

Can you find two other ways to make a shadow sharper?

Light Sources and Shadows LESSON 2

To make a shadow, you need light from something. You also need something to get in the way of the light. It must block the light.

Which of these things can cause shadows?

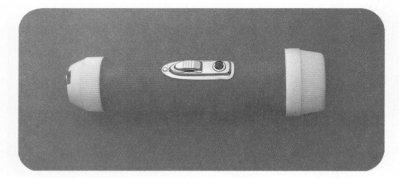

They all can!

Most of these things *produce* light. They give off light of their own. They are *light sources*.

However, two of the things do not produce their own light. One of these is the mirror.

A mirror is not a source of light. But it can *reflect* light that comes from some light source.

Which other thing reflects light instead of producing its own? Have you ever seen a shadow caused by this object?

A simple light source. Here is a light source that is easy to make.

It can be made with these materials.

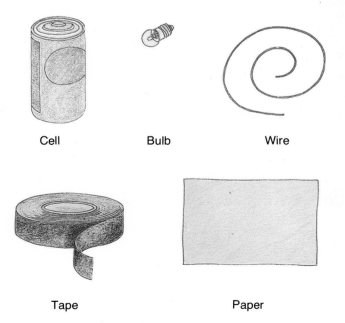

Cell   Bulb   Wire

Tape   Paper

Here are the steps for putting it together.

1. Wind the middle of the wire around the metal base of the bulb. Twist it tightly.

2. Hold the bottom of the bulb against the top of the cell. Bend the wire down the sides of the cell.

3. Tape the wire tightly to the sides of the cell. The bottom of the bulb should touch the top of the cell.

4. Tape both ends of the wire tightly to the bottom of the cell. The bulb should light.

5. Slip a piece of paper under the bulb. The bulb should go off.

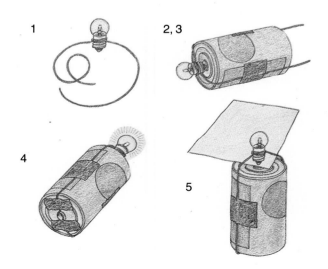

1   2, 3

4   5

Do all shadows made from one light source fall in the same direction? Find out what happens when you move the light source. Can you change the direction of a shadow?

1. Stick a pin into a piece of cardboard. Be sure that the pin stands straight up. Darken the room. Shine light on the pin. Find its shadow on the cardboard.

How long is the longest shadow the pin can make? How short is the shortest shadow?

Where is the light source when the pin's shadow is shortest? Where is it when the shadow is longest?

2. Stick a second pin into the cardboard. Make both pins cast shadows.

Where do the shadows fall? Can you make them fall in nearly the same direction? Can you make them cross? Can you get the two pins to cast only one shadow?

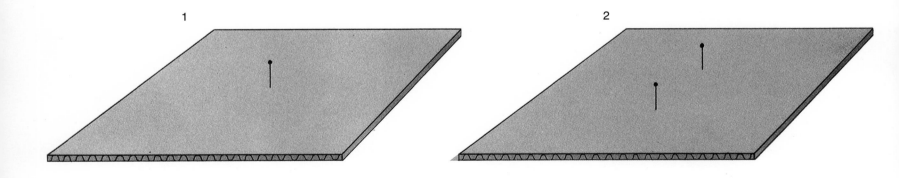

3. Now draw a circle on the cardboard. Stick eight pins along the circle. Make them cast shadows.

Can you make the shadows fall in the same direction? Can you make them all fall outside the circle? Can you make them all fall inside the circle?

What do you observe about the way shadows fall? Do shadows fall toward the light or away from it?

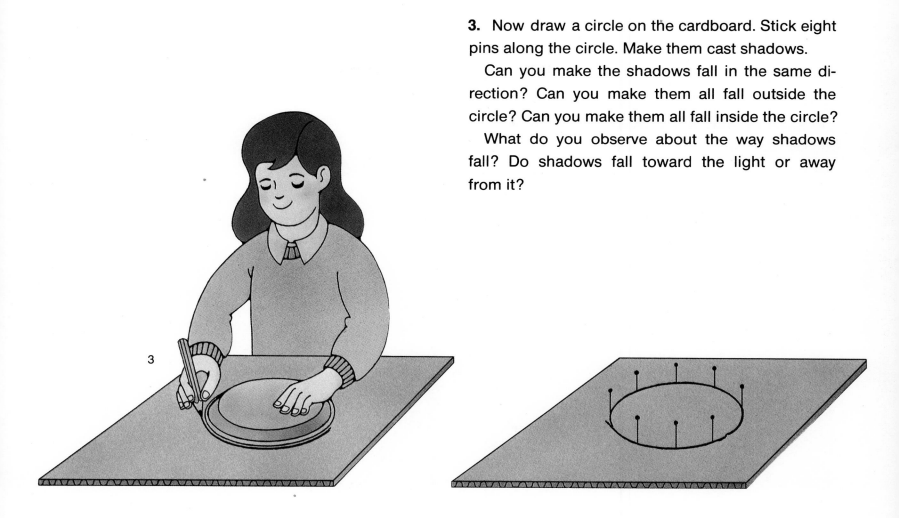

3

More than one light source. With one light source, how many shadows does an object cast? With two light sources, how many shadows does an object cast?

Can one object cast three shadows? How could you make this happen?

Could you make one object cast 10 shadows? More than 10? How could you do this?

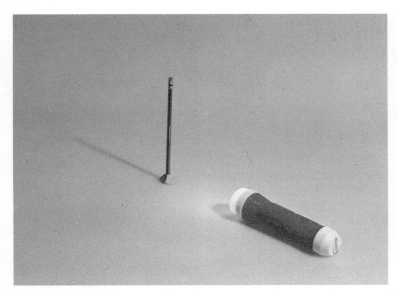

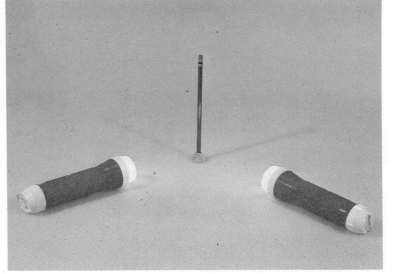

Can objects make shadows on themselves?

One object often blocks light from a second object. This causes a shadow on the second object. But can an object make a shadow on itself?

Stand in bright sunlight, facing a friend. Turn him or her around until your friend's nose casts a shadow across his or her face. **Safety Note:** *Never look directly at the sun.*

Can you make this shadow shorter or longer by turning your friend? Can you make it change from one side of the face to the other?

Now turn your friend until her or his whole face is in shadow. What object do you think is making this shadow?

What makes the shadow on this ball? Is it cast by any other object?

What part of the ball is in shadow? What part of the ball is blocking the light? What, then, is making the shadow on the ball?

How much of the ball is in shadow? By turning the ball, could you change the amount of shadow?

135

Sharp and Fuzzy Shadows LESSON 3

SOMETHING TO TRY

1. Here is a good way to compare shadows.

You will need a flat piece of clear glass or plastic. The glass from a small picture frame works well. **Safety Note:** *Put tape all around its edges. Then, you won't get cut.*

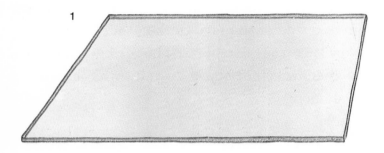

Now cut out a tiny piece of black paper or aluminum foil. Glue this to the center of the glass.

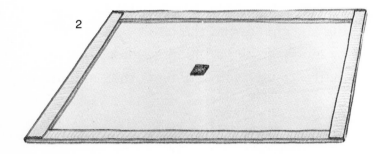

Fold a white card as shown to make a screen.

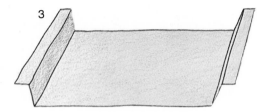

Tape the side edges to the glass. This distance between the screen and the glass should be about 1 cm.

Now hold the glass so that it faces a source of light. Look for the shadow of the paper or foil on the screen.

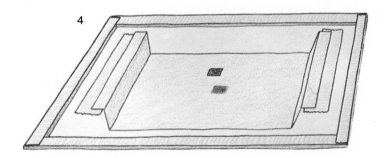

Use your shadow tester to compare the shadows made by different sources of light.

2. Here are two light sources. The small one is like the one shown on page 131. The large one is like a table lamp with its shade off. Which do you predict will make sharper shadows?

Use your shadow tester to find out. Make a fair test to see which light source makes the sharper shadows. In a fair test, everything must be the same except for one thing.

Shades and shadows. Most lamps in homes have shades. Suppose you took the shades off. Would the shadows made by these lamps be different? If so, in what way?

These two light sources are alike in every way except one. The light source in the bottom picture has a paper shade.

Which light source do you predict will make the sharper shadow?

Test your prediction in a darkened room. You can use your shadow tester instead of the pencil. Make the test fair. Keep everything the same except for the thing being tested.

What makes the shadows different? The two light sources are really not the same size. The one with the shade is larger. Its bulb lights up the shade. Then the shade itself becomes the light source!

SCIENCE PROJECT IDEA:
STUDYING SHADOWS AND SHADES

What are the shadows like in your home? Use your shadow tester to observe and compare them.

Compare the shadows made by the following kinds of light:

- a lamp with two bulbs, both bulbs lit
- a lamp with two bulbs, one bulb lit

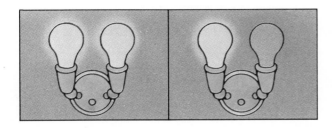

- a lamp with a shade on it
- the same lamp without the shade

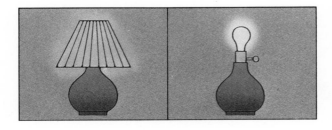

- a lamp with a white glass bowl
- the same lamp without the bowl

- an ordinary electric light bulb
- a long glass, electric light tube

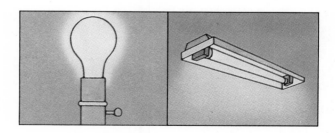

To compare the shadows fairly, what must you keep the same?

Which lights do you think are best for writing? Why? Which are best for taking out a splinter? Why? Which are best for sitting and talking? Why?

Dark and Light Shadows LESSON 4

SOMETHING TO TRY

1. See if a clear plastic bag casts a shadow. If so, does blowing air into the bag make the shadow any darker or brighter? Does filling the bag with scrap paper make any difference?

2. Find out if a clear tumbler will cast a shadow. If it does, will filling the tumbler with water make the shadow any darker or lighter?

Using a straw, blow bubbles in the water. Do these air bubbles cast shadows?

3. Set a clear container over white paper in bright sunlight. Fill it with water. Then poke a pencil in and out of the water to make ripples. Do these ripples cast shadows on the paper?

Will a hair floating on the water cast a shadow?

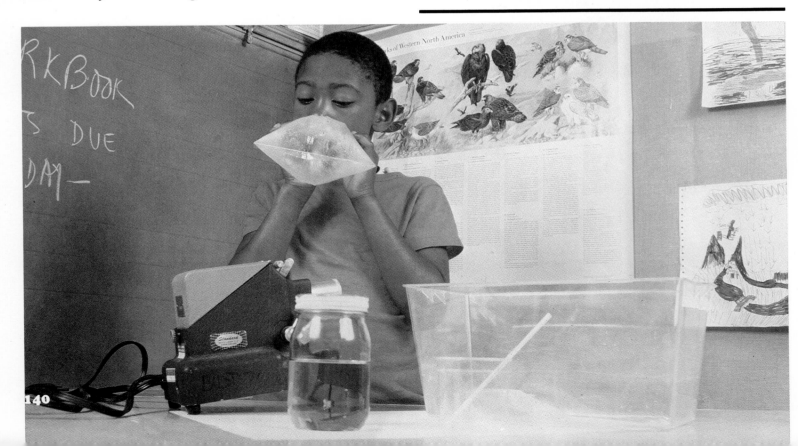

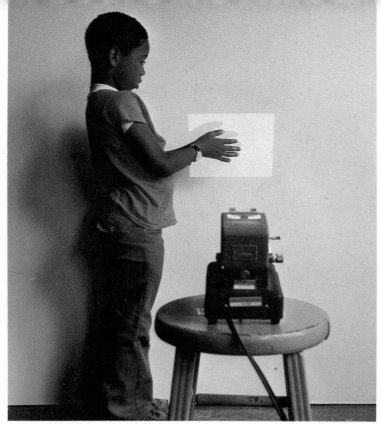

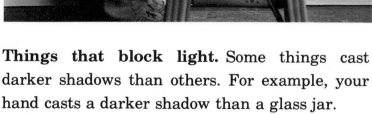

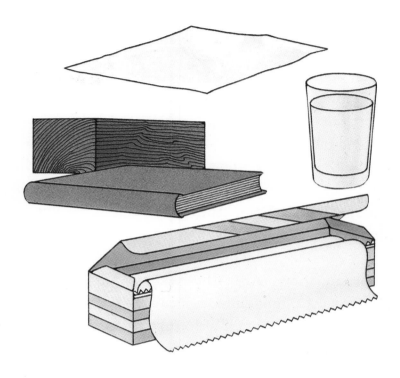

Things that block light. Some things cast darker shadows than others. For example, your hand casts a darker shadow than a glass jar.

The darkest shadows are cast by things that block all light. These things are called *opaque*. A book is opaque. So is a block of wood. Is a piece of cardboard opaque?

Things that let light through. Some things cast shadows that you can hardly see. Good examples are clear glass, clean water, and ice.

These things let a lot of light through. Because you can see through them clearly, such things are called *transparent*.

What is the thickest transparent thing you can think of? Is it a solid, liquid, or gas?

Some other things let light through, but you cannot see through them clearly. Such things are called *translucent*. Wax paper is translucent. So is most other paper. What other translucent things can you find? What are their shadows like?

Shadows made by X-rays. You know that your body can cast a shadow. But did you know that there is a way to make just your bones cast shadows?

Almost 100 years ago, a scientist in Germany named Wilhelm Konrad Roentgen discovered rays that no one knew about before. At first, he did not know what the rays were, so he called them *X-rays.* Later, they also came to be known as *Roentgen rays.*

X-rays are a lot like light. However, you cannot see them. Also, they can go through some things that light cannot go through. For example, they can go through skin and flesh. They make bones and teeth cast shadows.

Doctors and dentists use X-rays to make shadows. They can see these shadows by using special screens or taking pictures. The shadows can show whether you have a broken bone or whether your new tooth will grow in straight.

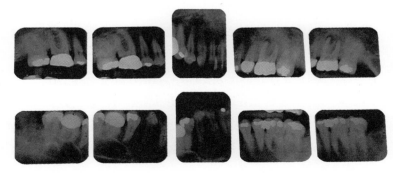

JOBS Using Science

Shadows in photos. The left-hand photo was taken indoors in bright light. There is a dark and sharp shadow on the child's face. What cast this shadow?

The right-hand photo shows the same child in the same place. But this time someone held a sheet of white cardboard nearby. The cardboard reflected light into the shadow. Which photo do you like better?

Sometimes it is good to have dark and sharp shadows in a photo. They can show bumps and hollows and whether things are rough or smooth. Other times shadows can spoil a picture.

Photographers often spend time moving lights and objects that reflect light before taking a picture. To get sharp shadows they may use a small light source. To get lighter and fuzzier shadows they may use a larger light source. Look at the umbrella lamp shown here. How else can they make shadows lighter and fuzzier?

Ideas for REVIEW

- To make a shadow you need light and an object that blocks this light.

- The size, shape, and position of a shadow on a screen may be changed by
  - moving the object.
  - moving the screen.
  - moving the light source.

- A shadow becomes larger when the object is moved farther from the screen.

- A shadow becomes sharper when the object is closer to the screen.

- The smaller the light source, the sharper an object's shadow.

- Some objects produce light, but most reflect light from a light source.

- Opaque things block all light and thus cast the darkest shadows.

- Transparent things let light through. Therefore you can see through them clearly.

- Translucent things let light through, but you cannot see through them clearly.

- Shadows may be made lighter by shining or reflecting light into them.

TEST Your Understanding

Choose the picture or words that best answer each question. Write the letter of your answer on a piece of paper. *Do not write in this book.*

1. Suppose you have a flashlight, a ruler, and a screen. How would you make the ruler cast its shadow on the screen?
   a. Hold the flashlight between the ruler and the screen.
   b. Hold the ruler between the flashlight and the screen.
   c. Put the screen between the ruler and the flashlight.

2. To make a shadow larger you can move
   a. the object closer to the screen
   b. the object closer to the light source
   c. the light source farther from the screen

3. Which of these does NOT produce light?

4. Which picture best shows where the shadow cast by the pin would be?

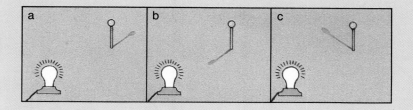

5. Taking off a lamp shade will make shadows
   a. lighter   c. sharper
   b. fuzzier   d. smaller

6. Which of these will cast the lightest shadow in a fair test?

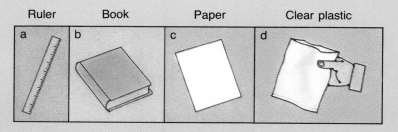

7. Which of these will cast the darkest shadow in a fair test?
   a. piece of clear glass   c. hand
   b. sheet of wax paper   d. water in clear glass

PROBLEMS

1. Sun shadows. Where was the sun when each of the pictures below was taken? How can you tell?

2. Shadow shapes. The drawings below show four shadows and five blocks. Which block or blocks could have made each shadow?

1   2   3   4   a   b   c   d   e

3. A shadow on the moon. Once in a while, the earth casts a shadow on the moon. Then we say there is an *eclipse* of the moon. What could be the light source that causes this shadow? Draw a picture of an eclipse of the moon. Label the earth, the moon, and the light source.

FIND OUT on Your Own

Most shadows appear to be gray or black. Have you ever seen a colored shadow?

How could you make a colored shadow? Which of these would you use?

- a colored light, such as a red or blue Christmas tree light

- a colored opaque object, such as a yellow or purple book

- a colored transparent object, such as a green or brown bottle

- a colored surface for the shadow to fall on, such as a piece of orange or yellow paper

Now try some experiments to see if you can make colored shadows. What do you find?

7 Sunlight on the Earth and Moon

On clear days the sun shines on the ground. But many things block the sunlight and cast shadows. What things are casting shadows in this picture? Which of these are moving? Do their shadows move with them? Which are standing still? Do their shadows stand still, too?

Why don't we have sunlight all the time—at night, too? Can you think of something that does get sunlight at night?

149

Sunlight and Shadows LESSON 1

SOMETHING TO TRY

Go outdoors on a sunny day. Find a pole that casts a shadow or hammer a long stick into the ground. Mark the tip of its shadow. Then record the time. Where do you predict the tip of the shadow will be after 15 minutes? Mark the place. Ask some of your classmates to mark where they predict it will be.

Now, wait exactly 15 minutes. Where is the tip of the shadow? Did anyone predict the right place?

Try this again. Also predict where the shadow will be after 30 minutes, after 1 hour. Then test your predictions.

What does the shadow do? How might you explain this?

Why shadows change. On a sunny day the shadows of objects keep changing. Why is this?

Could it be because
- the objects move?
- the sun moves?
- the earth moves?
- more than one thing moves?

Of course trees, houses, and poles are fastened to the earth. Their shadows cannot change unless the earth moves, or the sun moves.

Do you know which moves? Is it the sun or earth that moves? Could it be both?

This is an easy question if you know the answer. But it is not easy to prove the answer!

You may have heard that the earth moves—that the sun only seems to move. This is true.

But how can you be sure? How can people prove that the earth moves?

A record of the sun's position. Some students made a record of the sun's position in the sky.

First, they stuck a lump of clay on a step outdoors. They chose a sunny spot where no one would walk.

Next, they stuck a drinking straw into the clay so that it made no shadow. To have no shadow the straw had to point directly at the sun.

Safety Note: *It is important that you do not look directly at the sun.*

One hour later, the straw did cast a shadow. How can you explain this?

Then, the students stuck a second straw into the clay. Again, they pointed it toward the sun so that it cast no shadow. They were careful not to move the first straw. Why do you think they had to be careful not to move the first straw?

In this way, they added a new straw every hour. The straws showed how the sun's position in the sky changed.

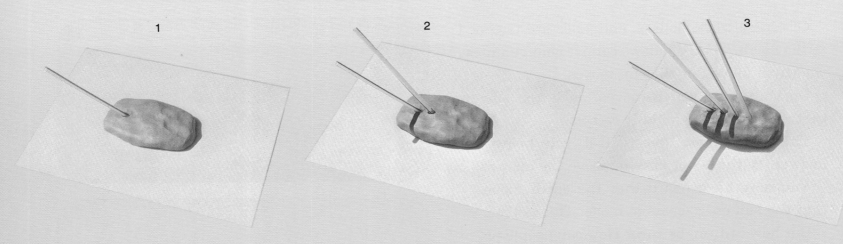

The Moving Earth LESSON 2

How can you tell whether something is moving? How can you tell whether you are moving?

Sometimes it is not easy to be sure!

For example, suppose you are in a school bus, looking out. There is another bus next to yours. If one bus moves, can you always tell right away which one is moving? Do you sometimes get fooled?

This is a little like observing the sun. You know the sun seems to change its position in the sky. But is this because the sun is moving?

Or is it because the whole earth, with you on it, is moving?

You easily can tell whether your bus is moving. You can watch trees and buildings. If these seem to move, it must be that your bus is moving.

But what can you look at to find out whether the earth is moving?

You can watch the stars. But can you be sure that they are standing still?

No! You have to use other ways to prove that the earth is moving!

153

The earth from space. Many pictures of the earth have been taken from space. The pictures show that the earth is round, like a giant ball. They show the earth's land and water. They show clouds in the air around the earth.

From a spaceship, can astronauts tell whether the earth is moving? From far out in space, they might be able to watch it move.

How can astronauts be sure that the earth is moving? If their spaceship is moving, they might not be able to tell.

One clue to the earth's motion is seen in photographs. Scientists study the photographs taken from space. They can see that the clouds seem to form *swirls* around the earth.

Clouds mark the path of moving air. They can show the direction of the wind. They can show that the wind blows along curved paths of the earth.

Why does the wind blow along curved paths? Why doesn't it blow along straight paths?

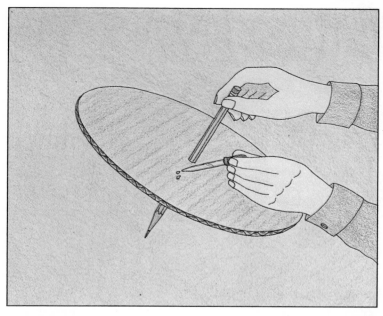

Why do winds tend to blow along curved paths on the earth?

Find a piece of cardboard, at least 20 cm by 20 cm. Pin one end of a straw to the center. Make a mark on the straw 10 cm from the pin. Push a pencil through the straw at this mark and draw a circle. Then cut the cardboard along this circle.

Next, put several drops of water on the cardboard. Put them right next to the pencil. Then, without turning the cardboard, tilt it so that the water runs down across it. What kind of path does the water make—straight or curved?

Try this a few times. Does the same thing happen each time?

Then try turning the cardboard while the water runs down across it. What kind of path does the water make—straight or curved?

Try this in different ways. Put the water in different places on the cardboard. Tilt the cardboard a lot or a little. Turn it in different directions and at different speeds. What do you observe?

Moving air would tend to do the same thing as the water. Winds are moving air. As winds move across the earth, they make curved paths marked by swirls of clouds. What do these paths show?

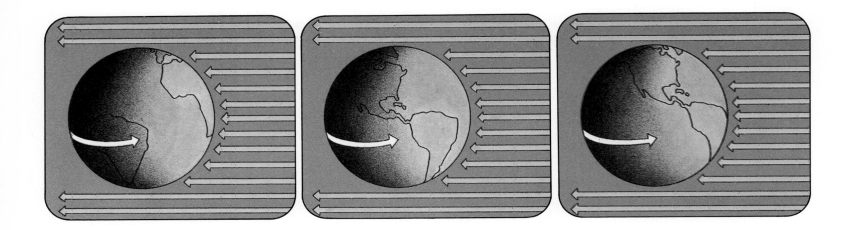

The sun's changing position. How many times can a record turn around in a minute? How many times could it turn around in a day? You probably have guessed that it could turn around a great many times!

The earth turns around just once in a whole day—24 hours. It turns around steadily.

We can't feel the earth turn. To us, it seems to be standing still. The sun appears to move instead. It seems to rise in the morning and set in the evening.

The turning of the earth makes the sun appear to move across the sky.

The moon's changing position. The sun seems to move because the earth turns. The moon also seems to move because the earth turns. The moon moves around the earth once a month. Since the earth is moving too, the moon rises at a different time each night.

The stars seem to move, too, because the earth is moving. They are like our sun, but they are very far away.

SOMETHING TO THINK ABOUT

The girl in the picture is trying to find out how the moon moves across the sky. She is going to look at the moon every half hour to see what happens. She wants to compare the position of the moon with the position of another object. What object has she chosen?

What must the girl be careful to do each time she goes outside to look at the moon?

What do you think will happen?

How can you find out?

Day and Night   LESSON 3

This picture shows a city in the late afternoon. Why are the shadows so long? As the earth keeps turning, the shadows get longer and longer. They cover more and more of the ground.

Slowly the sun seems to sink lower in the sky. Soon it will be hidden by the mountains.

Most of the flat ground is all in shadow. The earth blocks the sunlight. It causes a shadow on itself!

The earth, with you on it, keeps turning around—once every day. When it has turned far enough, you can no longer see the sun. Then you say the sun has "set." But the sun is still shining on other parts of the earth!

While you are sleeping, children in some places are playing outdoors in sunlight.

It is always daytime somewhere on the earth. It is always nighttime somewhere else on the earth. The sun always seems to be rising somewhere, and setting somewhere else.

SOMETHING TO TRY

What causes daytime and nighttime?

Here is a way of finding out. Darken the room except for a single electric light. Fasten a ball to a piece of string. Holding the string, move the ball 1 m from the light.

How much of the ball is in the light? How much is in shadow? What causes this shadow?

Try this with balls of different sizes. Do they all have the same amount in light and in shadow?

Does the amount in light and in shadow change when you move a ball? Does it change when you turn a ball around?

The earth is round, like a giant ball. It is always in the light of the sun. But, at any time, only part of it is in direct sunlight.

This part of the earth has daytime. The other part has nighttime because it is in shadow. What causes the shadow?

SCIENCE PROJECT IDEA:
SEEING THE EARTH FROM SPACE

Stand a globe outdoors in the sun. Point the *North Pole* toward the north. Use a book to prop up the globe. The globe should be tilted and turned so that your home area is at the top.

A globe is a tiny model of the earth. How much of the model is in direct sunlight?

On the model, is your home area in direct sunlight? Is it the same on the real earth?

What part of the model is in shadow? Suppose you could see the earth from space. Do you think the same part of the real earth would be in shadow?

Stick a piece of clay over your home area at the top of the globe. Stand a toothpick straight up in the clay. Observe where the shadow falls.

Look around you at the shadows on the real earth. Where do they fall? Do they point in the same direction as the toothpick's shadow on the globe?

When you turn the model earth, does the toothpick's shadow change? Can you make your home area go from "day" to "night"? Can you make the sun "rise" and "set"?

Moving into shadow. Suppose you live in Montreal, Quebec. One evening, right after dark, you call your grandfather in Los Angeles, California. He tells you that it is still daylight in Los Angeles. The sun is still shining there.

This is because Montreal is in the earth's shadow, but Los Angeles is not. The earth has not turned far enough to bring Los Angeles into the shadow. This will take about three more hours.

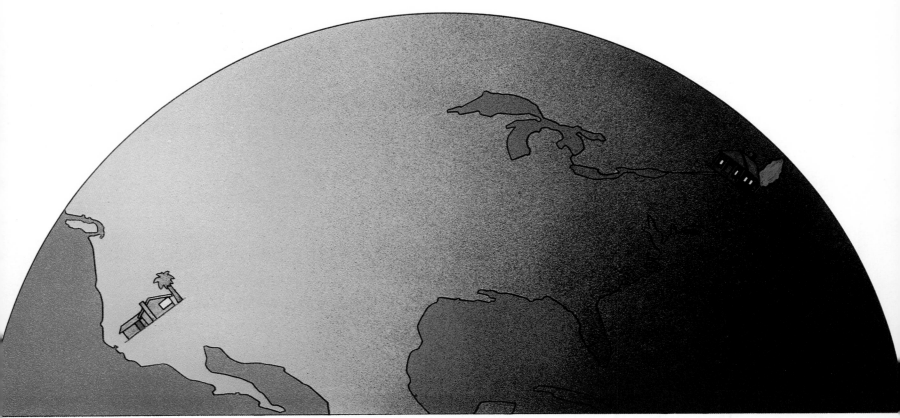

The clocks in this picture show the time in different cities: PEKING, HONG KONG, PHNOM PENH, GUAM, PALO ALTO, MEMPHIS, FORT.

JOBS Using Science

The clocks in this picture show the time in different cities. You can see clocks like these at some airports, hotels, or television stations.

People who work in these places often look at these clocks. So do people who travel. They need to know what time it is in different parts of the earth.

Why is the time different in different parts of the earth? How could you tell from clocks like these whether people in different places are probably sleeping? How could you tell whether they are in school or at work?

Light on the Earth LESSON 4

How much of the earth are you able to see? Can you see any more of it from a tall building or a high hill?

How much of it could you see from an airplane? How much of it might you see from a spaceship?

Since you can see the earth, your eyes must be getting light from it. Does the earth give off light because it is hot, like a fire?

Or, does it mostly reflect light that comes from another source?

If the earth reflects light, from what source does most of this light come?

A problem. How do these two pictures show that the earth reflects sunlight? Do all the lights in the city make as much light as the sun does?

Daylight. In the daytime, just about everything you see outdoors reflects sunlight. That is why you are able to see well in daylight.

Even so, many things that you see in daylight do not get direct sunlight. You can see them even when they are in shadow. You can even see things indoors without the lights on. Why is this?

It is because these things get sunlight, even though it is not direct. They get sunlight that is reflected by other objects, such as trees, clouds, and buildings. Then they, in turn, reflect this reflected sunlight.

SOMETHING TO TRY

After sunset, how long does it take for the sky to get really dark?

On a clear day, watch for the sun to set. Write down the time. **Safety Note:** *Never look directly at the sun.* *Look a little distance away from it.*

After the sun sets, how long can you read outdoors without a light? Keep track of the time.

Try reading at sunset on different days. What do you find?

After sunset, the sun is hidden by the earth. It can no longer be seen. Even so, there is still enough light to see by for awhile. It is called *twilight.*

Is there twilight in the morning before the sun rises? How could you find out?

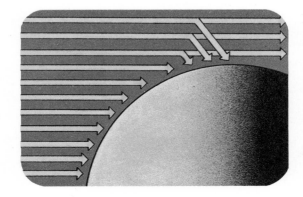

Twilight is caused by light from the sun. But the light does not come directly from the sun. It is reflected by tiny particles high up in the air.

Some of the reflecting particles are water or ice. Some are dust. The particles act like tiny mirrors. They reflect some of the sunlight to the dark side of the earth, which causes twilight.

165

Sunlight on the Moon LESSON 5

You have seen how the moon seems to change its shape. Sometimes it looks round. Sometimes it looks like the edge of your fingernail.

Think about the different shapes that the moon seems to have. Look at the ten shapes below. Which shapes match the different shapes of the moon?

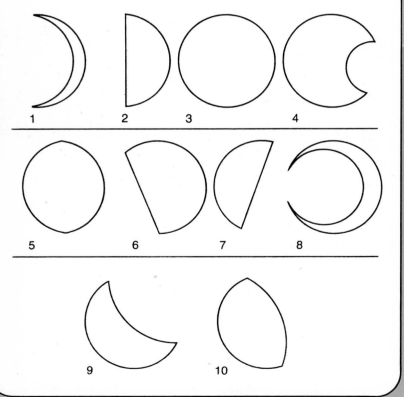

SOMETHING TO TRY

Why does the moon show different shapes? Can you find the moon in the daytime? Keep looking every day until you see it.

When you find the moon, observe the shape it seems to have. Which of the shapes shown on this page does the moon look like?

Stand in a sunny place and hold up a ball. Notice the part of the ball that is in sunlight. How much of this sunlit part can you see? Half of it? Less than half of it? More than half of it? Does the amount in sunlight change when you move the ball?

Next, hold the ball so that it is directly between you and the moon. Look at the ball. Then look at the moon. Does the sunlit part of the ball look like the moon?

Suppose the moon were in a different position in the sky. What would it look like in this new position? Make a prediction. Test your prediction by holding the ball in the new position.

What the moon looks like. The moon is like a giant ball in sunlight. It gets direct sunlight on only one side. The other side is in shadow.

At different times we see different amounts of the moon's sunlit side. But we usually cannot see any of the side in shadow.

Often we see less than half of the moon's sunlit side. Then we say that there is a *crescent moon*.

At other times we see only half of the sunlit side of the moon. We call this a *half moon*.

Sometimes we see more than half, but not all, of the moon's sunlit side. We call this moon a *gibbous moon*.

Sometimes the sunlit side of the moon is facing us. Then we can see all of this sunlit side. We say that there is a *full moon*.

SCIENCE PROJECT IDEA:
RECORDING MOON CHANGES

Your class can keep a record of the moon's shape for a week or two. Take turns looking for the moon each day. Carefully draw its shape as you see it. Do this on white paper. Cut it out and paste it on a square of dark paper. Then add the date.

Look at the shapes carefully. Does the moon's shape seem to change in a regular way, as in "A"? Or does it seem to skip around, as in "B"?

From your record can you tell how many days the moon takes to go from half to full ?

Or can you tell how long the moon takes to go from full to half ? How long do you suppose it would take to go from full to full ?

The time between a full moon and the next full moon was once called a "moon." It is about 29 days. Our word "month" came from "moon." But on the calendars, the months that we use today are not the same as "moons."

Why do you suppose the moon's shape appears to change in a regular way?

SOMETHING TO TRY

Try this in a darkened room with a single electric light in it. Hold up a ball so that light falls on it. Keep it out of your shadow. It may help to stick a sharp pencil into the ball.

In what position must you hold the ball to see

- all of its lighted side?

- none of its lighted side?

- half of its lighted side?

Now imagine that the ball is a model of the moon. Pretend that your head is the earth and the light is the sun. Now, in what position must you hold the model moon to see a "full moon"? A "gibbous moon"? A "half moon"? A "crescent moon"?

Next, move the model moon around you in a circle. Try to keep it out of your shadow. As you do this, what change do you see in the lighted part?

Can you make the model moon seem to go from crescent to half to gibbous to full? Then can you make it seem to go back to gibbous, half, and crescent?

Holding the model moon, turn away from the sun. As you turn, does the lighted part seem to get larger or smaller? What happens to the model when you turn toward the sun?

Ideas for REVIEW

- Shadows cast by objects in sunlight move.

- This shows that the sun, the earth, or both must move.

- As seen from far off in space, the earth looks like a giant ball in sunlight.

- Moving things tend to make curved paths on an object that is turning.

- The curved paths of winds on the earth show that the earth is turning.

- Because the earth turns, the sun appears to move across the sky.

- Because the earth turns, the moon and stars also appear to move across the sky.

- One side of the earth is in sunlight and has daytime. At the same time, the other side is in shadow and has nighttime.

- We are able to see most objects because they reflect light.

- The moon gets sunlight on one side. At the same time, its other side is in shadow.

- The moon's shape seems to change because we see different amounts of the moon's sunlit side.

TEST Your Understanding

On a piece of paper, write the best answer to each of the following questions. *Do not write in this book.*

1. On sunny days, the shadows of people are shortest

    a. in the early morning

    b. at about noon

    c. in the late afternoon

2. It gets dark at night because

    a. the place where we live moves into the earth's shadow

    b. the sun moves around to the other side of the earth

    c. the sun stops shining

3. If the earth turned around any faster,

    a. the sun would seem to stand still in the sky

    b. days would be shorter than they are now

    c. nights would be longer than they are now

4. If light could not be reflected, we would still have

    a. moonlight

    b. twilight

    c. sunlight

5. When the moon appears as a crescent in the sky

    a. half of the moon is in sunlight

    b. less than half of the moon is in sunlight

    c. the whole sunlit side of the moon is facing the earth

PROBLEMS

1. Moon Shapes

The drawings to the right show different positions that the moon, earth, and sun may have.

Imagine that

this is you.

this is the earth.

this is the moon.

this is sunlight—the sun is a long way off at the right.

Imagine that you are standing on the earth, as shown in drawing A. What would the moon look like to you? What would it look like to you as shown in drawing B? As shown in drawing C?

Match the letter of each drawing with the shape of the moon you would see in the sky.

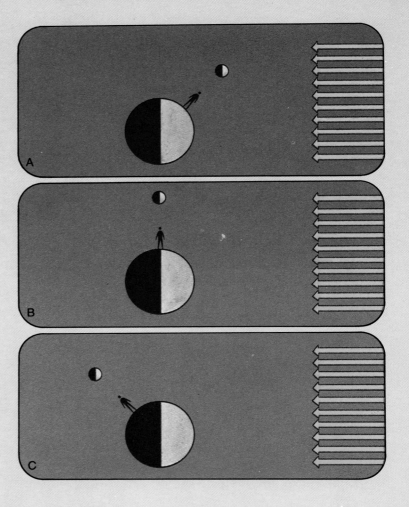

A

B

C

1   Crescent

2   Half

3   Gibbous

4   Full

2. Shadow Movement

Would the shadow of the tree move

- if the sun stood still and the earth turned?

- if the earth stood still and the sun moved?

- if both the earth and sun moved like this?

FIND OUT on Your Own

On a clear night when there is a crescent moon, you can see something interesting. You can see the crescent moon. But you also may make out a part of the moon that is in shadow. Then you can see all of the moon that faces the earth!

Something must be making the shadow lighter. What is doing this? You can check your ideas by making models of the earth, moon, and sun.

8 Heat and Temperature

Taking temperature is important to many people. Why is it important to a doctor? A baker? Why is it important to you?

It is useful to know what the temperature is now. Sometimes it is useful to know what it will be. How could knowing this be useful to you?

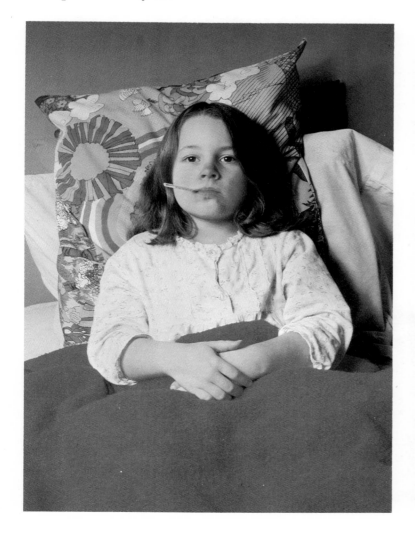

One Way to Tell Temperature

LESSON 1

Our skin helps us tell whether something is hot or cold. It also helps us tell whether one thing is warmer or cooler than another. But how well can our skin tell small differences in temperature?

SOMETHING TO TRY

1. Fill two paper cups with warm water. Make the water in one of the cups warmer than the water in the other. Have a partner put a finger in each cup. Ask which seems warmer. Have your partner change hands and feel the water again. Which seems warmer this time?

Now you try it. Can you tell which cup holds the warmer water?

2. Set the cups of water on opposite sides of the room. Have your partner dip a finger in one cup and then go dip a finger in the other. Can your partner tell which is warmer? You try it. Can you tell which is warmer?

Is it easy to remember how warm something feels? How long can you remember how warm or cold something feels after you have moved away from it?

Observing Temperature Changes

LESSON 2

Our skin helps us tell temperature. But our skin can be fooled. Also, our skin does not remember very well. It is not reliable. There are better ways to tell temperature.

How can the girl in the picture tell where the wall ends without looking?

SOMETHING TO TRY

Dip the opening of a frozen juice can in some detergent. Turn the can upright. A thin *film* of liquid should cover the opening.

Set the can in some warm water. What happens to the film?

When the film breaks, let the can cool. Then try this again and again. Are your observations the same each time?

What do you think happens to the air inside the can as it warms?

SCIENCE PROJECT IDEA:
MAKING AN AIR THERMOMETER

A simple *thermometer* can be made from things found in your home or classroom. Find a bottle with a long, narrow neck. Put a strip of masking tape on the neck of the bottle as shown in the picture. Then tape the bottle to a block of wood. Pour some colored water into a pie tin so that it is about 2 cm deep.

When everything is ready, hold your hands around the bottle to warm it. You might need some friends' hands to help you. As soon as the bottle is warm, quickly turn it upside down and put it in the pan. Your thermometer should look like the one in the picture.

As the air in the bottle cools, what happens to the level of the colored water? If you warm the air in the bottle again, what do you think will happen? Test your prediction.

In order to read your thermometer, you need a scale. Find out how to make a scale on the next page.

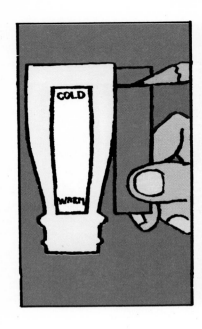   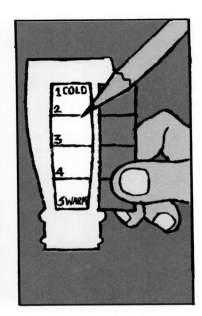

The drawings above show you what a scale looks like. Put your thermometer in a warm place for a half hour. When it stops moving, mark the level of the colored water "WARM."

Next, put the thermometer in a cold place for a half hour. When it stops moving, mark the level of the colored water "COLD."

Make three marks, equally spaced, between "WARM" and "COLD." Number the marks from 1 to 5. Now your thermometer has a scale.

Put your thermometer someplace where you can see it. Record the level of the colored water at different times during the day.

Expanding air. The Science Project Idea showed how to make an air thermometer. Air makes it work. The thermometer shows changes in temperature. As the air inside the bottle gets warm, it *expands*. It takes up more space. It pushes some liquid out the neck. As the air inside the bottle cools, it *contracts*. It takes up less space. It lets liquid come up in the neck.

Gail's experiment. Gail wondered if liquids expand and contract with changes in temperature as much as air does. So she did an experiment.

First, she found three bottles like those in the picture. Using water colored red, she made one into an air thermometer. This would show how air in a bottle changes as the temperature changes.

Gail filled the second bottle with colored water. Then she filled the third with rubbing alcohol that had color added. She filled both bottles to the same level in the neck as the air thermometer.

She put a mark on each of the bottles to show how full it was. Then she put them in a cold place and waited a half hour. What did she observe?

Then Gail put the bottles in a warm place. After a half hour she examined them again. What did she observe?

Which material had expanded the most when warmed? Was it the same material that contracted most when cooled?

Changes in solids. The metal ball and ring in the pictures show how solids change when heated.

When the ball and ring are cool, the ball can easily fit through the ring.

What do you suppose happens to the ball when it is heated?

When the ball is hot, it will not go through the ring.

You know that liquids and gases expand when heated. They contract when cooled. Solids also expand when heated and contract when cooled. They do not change much, but you might notice some differences. A door might stick on hot days. Telephone wires sag on hot days. A toaster makes noises as it cools off.

Can you think of any other examples of solids expanding and contracting?

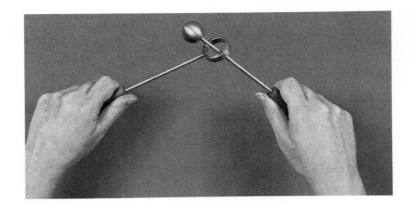

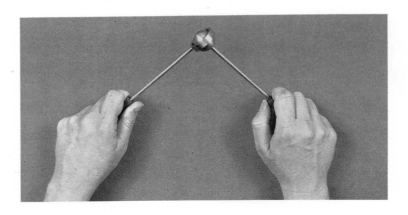

SOME THINGS TO THINK ABOUT

1. The tank was filled in the morning. By noon, a puddle appeared under the tank. How would you explain what happened?

2. The boy thinks a leak made his tire "soft." What else could it be?

3. Putting the jar lid under hot water loosened it. How could you explain this?

4. Many bridges have a space like this at each end. What do you think these spaces are for?

Thermometers LESSON 3

You know how some kinds of matter change when their temperatures change. They expand or contract. That is why they can be used in thermometers to show changes in temperature.

You already have made a thermometer that uses air. But most thermometers use liquids or solids. How do these thermometers work? Let's look again at a bottle filled with liquid.

SOMETHING TO TRY

Try to get two bottles like these. One should have a wide neck and the other a narrow neck. Fill them with colored water about half way up the necks. Mark the level of the liquid in each bottle. Then put them in a cold place. After two hours look at them. Which level changed more? What do you think caused that one to change more? Now put the bottles in a warm place. In two hours look at them again. Which bottle shows the greater change? Why? If you want a liquid level to change a lot for small temperature changes what shape container would you use?

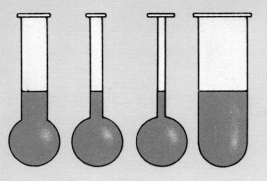

A problem. In the two bottles you observed, liquids expanded or contracted when their temperatures changed. The liquid levels changed when their temperatures changed. But they changed very little. One showed more change than the other.

Suppose that you wanted the liquid level to change more. Which shape of container would be best? Why?

Liquid-in-glass thermometers. Here are some liquid-in-glass thermometers. What happens to the level of the liquids as their temperatures change? What causes this change in liquid level?

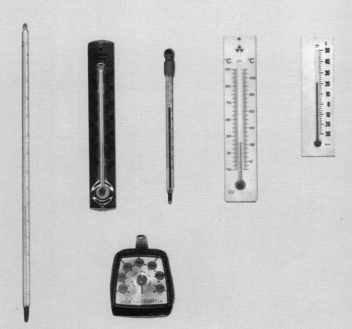

Solid thermometers. Some thermometers use solid materials instead of a liquid. This oven thermometer has a metal strip. It expands or contracts as its high temperature changes. This makes the needle move.

Why might a solid thermometer be better than a liquid-in-glass thermometer in an oven?

What would happen to some liquids in very hot places? In very cold places? What might happen to the glass that holds the liquid?

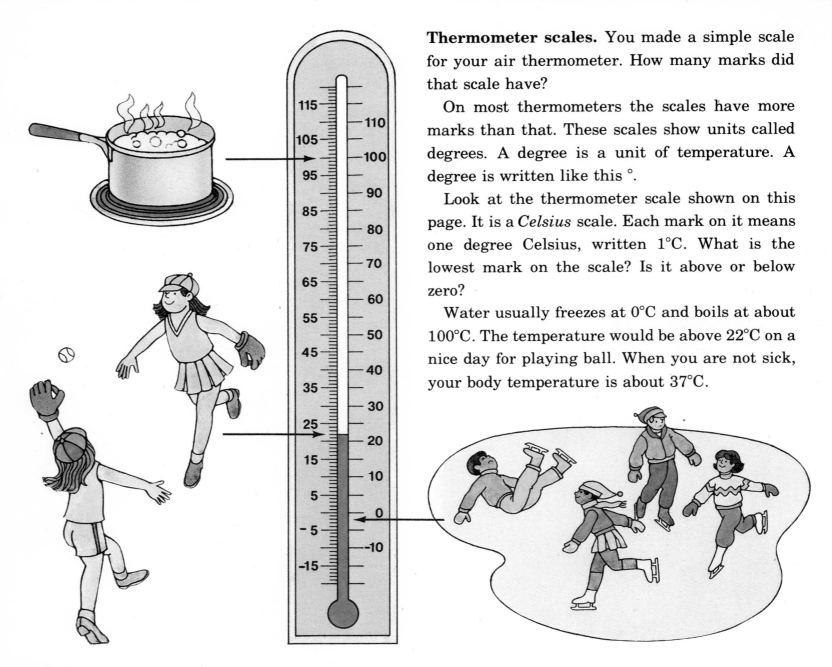

Thermometer scales. You made a simple scale for your air thermometer. How many marks did that scale have?

On most thermometers the scales have more marks than that. These scales show units called degrees. A degree is a unit of temperature. A degree is written like this °.

Look at the thermometer scale shown on this page. It is a *Celsius* scale. Each mark on it means one degree Celsius, written 1°C. What is the lowest mark on the scale? Is it above or below zero?

Water usually freezes at 0°C and boils at about 100°C. The temperature would be above 22°C on a nice day for playing ball. When you are not sick, your body temperature is about 37°C.

1. Fill an insulated cup with ice cubes. As they melt, take the temperature when the mixture is

- almost all ice
- mostly ice, some water
- mostly water, some ice
- only a tiny bit of ice left

How do these temperatures compare?

2. Put some more ice cubes in an insulated cup. Add 50 mL of table salt over the ice cubes. As they melt, take the temperature.

How does it compare with the temperature of only ice and water? Add more salt. Take the temperature a few minutes later. What is the lowest temperature you can get with an ice-and-salt mixture?

3. Fill an insulated cup with hot water from the tap. Before using a thermometer, estimate its temperature. Then measure its temperature. How does the temperature compare with your estimate?

4. Estimate the temperature of your classroom. Then check it with a thermometer. How good was your estimate? Try this outdoors, too.

Temperatures of Large and Small Things LESSON 4

Mr. Jones must be sure the milk is the right temperature. He tests it by shaking a drop on his wrist. Is the drop about the same temperature as the milk in the bottle?

Taking a sample. The person in the picture is testing a *sample* of water from the ocean. A sample is a small bit of something that is like a larger amount. The water in the can is like the part of the ocean near the boat. It has the same temperature as the ocean water.

Would this sample be like the water in all other parts of the ocean? What would happen to the sample if it were left in a warm place for an hour? Then would it be a fair test of the ocean's temperature?

190

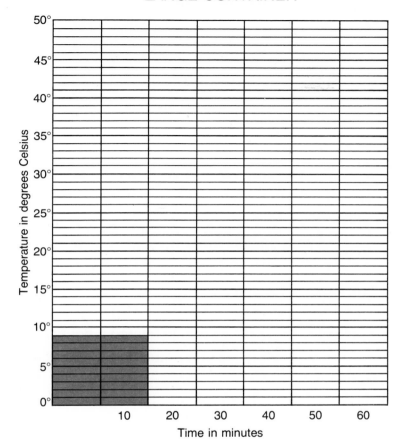

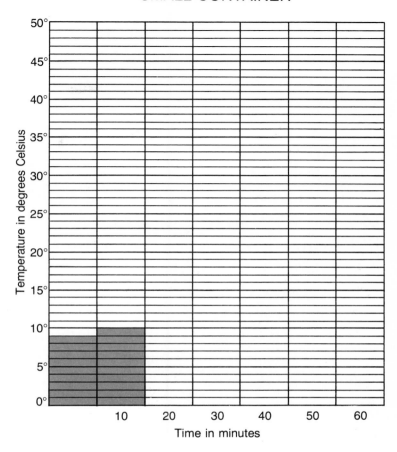

Amount and temperature change. Does a small sample of water warm up faster than a large amount? Does it cool faster? You can find out by testing two different amounts. Make two grids like those above.

Write "LARGE CONTAINER" at the top of one grid. Write "SMALL CONTAINER" at the top of the other. Write "temperature in degrees Celsius" along the left sides. Write "time in minutes" along the bottoms. Record your observations on the grids.

Fill a large container with the coldest tap water you can find. Dip out a small container of water. Set it beside the large container. Do you think it has the same temperature as the water in the large container? Will they both have the same temperature 10 minutes from now?

Take the temperature of the water in the large container. Record the temperature on your "LARGE CONTAINER" grid by coloring the first column.

Then take the temperature of the water in the small container. Record it on your "SMALL CONTAINER" grid by coloring the first column.

Are the two columns the same height? Is this what you thought would happen? After 10 minutes take both temperatures again.

Record them the same way in the 10-minute columns. What do they show?

Record both temperatures every 10 minutes for one hour.

At the end of the hour, look at all the columns on the grids. You now have two *bar graphs.* Each bar graph shows how temperatures changed as time passed.

Look at your graphs. What were the temperatures in both containers after 20 minutes? The temperatures after 40 minutes?

What do your observations show? Does a small sample of water cool faster than a large amount? Do you think that is true for other materials? How could you find out?

MAKING A PREDICTION

Suppose you did the same experiment with hot water. What do you predict would happen? What would the graphs look like? Try the experiment, using hot water. Record the temperatures on grids as you did for the cold water. How close are the results to your prediction?

Speeding and Slowing Temperature Changes LESSON 5

SOMETHING TO TRY

Here are two contests to have using ice cubes.

1. Melt a cube.

Have a race with the other groups in the class. See which group can melt their ice cube the fastest. Each group must begin at the same time. No group can use a fire. No group can break the ice cube into pieces. Think of ways that will help your ice cube melt quickly. You can use anything in the classroom to help you.

Which group was the winner? How did they melt their ice cube faster than the other groups?

2. Save a cube.

This time, see which group can keep their ice cube from melting. You can use paper, cloth, foil, plastic, and other things.

Write down the starting time. Quickly wrap up the ice cube to slow down its melting time. Write down how you wrapped it up. Peek at the ice cube every 5 minutes to see how much it has melted. Keep going until only one group has some ice left in the wrapper.

Which group's ice cube lasted the longest? What did they use to wrap it in?

Insulators and conductors. The team that kept its ice the longest used the best *insulator*. Their insulator let the smallest amount of heat reach the ice.

Wires in an iron get very hot. If a lot of heat moved through the handle, the handle could burn the person's hand. The handle must be a good insulator.

Most of the heat moves through the bottom of the iron to the clothing. The bottom is a good *conductor* of heat.

The bottom of a cooking pan must be a good conductor, too. Then heat from the stove can get to the food in the pan. But what about the handle? Should it be a good conductor or a good insulator? Look at the handles of some pans at home. Which are conductors? Which are insulators?

You will need a bowl of very hot water and some objects that are all about the same length. Some examples are

- an iron nail

- a small stick

- a plastic straw

- a piece of copper wire

- a rubber band

- a metal spoon

- a microscope slide

Which of these objects are good conductors of heat? Which are good insulators? Test each object to find out.

Ask several classmates to help. Each one should hold one end of an object. All together, put the other end in hot water. Everyone's fingers should be the same distance from the water.

As soon as an object feels hot, it should be pulled out. Record the order in which the objects are pulled out.

Try this several times. Each person should hold a different object each time. Record all results.

Which object is the best conductor of heat? Which is the best insulator?

Conductors. Most metals are good conductors of heat. Copper is one of them. You might have some pots and pans at home that have copper bottoms. Iron is also used for cookware, but it is not so good as copper. Silver is best, but it has a high price. Some pans that are made of metal have metal handles, too. To lift them from the stove, you need a potholder or a mitt. Insulated handles are safer because they don't burn you so easily.

Insulators. Things like glass, rubber, and plastic are good insulators. Not much heat moves through them. Lots of pans have plastic handles.

Air is a good insulator, too. Many materials have small air spaces. Look at all the holes full of air in a sweater or a piece of cloth.

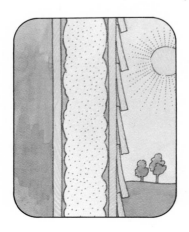

Some drinking cups are made of plastic foam. Plastic foam is made of bubbly, hot plastic that is hardened. There is air in each of the bubbles. A plastic foam cup can keep soup hot for a long time.

Home *insulation* has air bubbles in it, too. In the winter, an insulated house stays warm. In summer, it stays cool. Insulation saves energy.

What other things are insulated?

The thermometer. The thermometer was not invented by just one person. Like other inventions and discoveries, it took many people many years. Each person made the thermometer a little better.

In 1593, an Italian scientist named Galileo made a simple thermometer. It was a long-necked bottle that was open at the top. It had water in it. The water level was marked on the neck of the bottle. A person held the bottle in both hands. If they had a fever, the water level would rise above the mark.

Another Italian, The Grand Duke of Tuscany, made a thermometer in 1641. It was a lot like Galileo's, but it was closed. It had alcohol in it instead of water. Do you remember why alcohol works better than water?

In 1714, a German scientist named Gabriel Fahrenheit made a thermometer. He put mercury in it. Mercury doesn't boil so quickly as water and alcohol. It is better for measuring very high temperatures. Fahrenheit made a temperature scale. He called frozen seawater 0°. He called body temperature 100°. Water boils at 212°F.

In 1742, Anders Celsius, a Swedish astronomer, made up another temperature scale. He called the temperature of frozen freshwater 0°. He called the temperature of boiling water 100°.

Now, over 200 years later, the Fahrenheit scale or the Celsius scale is used all over the world.

JOBS Using Science

One house has snow on its roof. The other doesn't. How would you explain the difference?

Insulation can easily be put in new houses. It helps save heat energy in cold weather. Is it helpful in hot weather, too? Why do you think so?

These people are putting insulation in a refrigerator. It will keep out unwanted heat.

Older houses can be insulated, too. Then it will take less fuel to heat them. Does your home have insulation? How could you find out?

Ideas for REVIEW

- Often, skin is not reliable for telling the temperature of something.

- It is better to use a thermometer to tell temperature.

- Gases tend to expand when heated and contract when cooled.

- Most liquids and solids tend to expand when warmed and contract when cooled.

- Most common thermometers use liquids or solids. Thermometer scales are marked off in temperature units called degrees.

- On the Celsius scale, water usually freezes at 0° and boils at about 100°.

- When you are not sick, your body temperature is about 37°C.

- A small amount of water tends to cool faster and warm faster than a large amount.

- An insulator lets little heat move through it.

- A conductor lets much heat move through it.

- Metals usually are good conductors.

- Materials with air spaces usually are good insulators.

TEST Your Understanding

A. Choose the word or words that make each correct. Write your answers on a piece of paper. *Do not write in this book.*

1. On hot days, power lines usually sag (more, less) than on cold days.

2. Suppose someone buys a litre of gasoline. It is cold because it was pumped from a tank underground. As it warms, there will be (more, less) than a litre of gasoline.

3. Which of these is a good conductor of heat? (aluminum foil, plastic wrap, newspaper)

4. Suppose a doctor takes your temperature. It is 39.5°C. Would you have a fever? (yes, no)

5. Suppose alcohol bursts into flame if its temperature rises to 150°C. Would it be safe to warm alcohol by surrounding it with boiling water? (yes, no)

B. Choose a word from Column B that best matches the words in Column A. On a piece of paper, write the letter of the word next to the number it matches.

A	B
6. used to measure temperature	**a.** silver
7. stands for degrees Celsius	**b.** scale
8. marked off in degrees	**c.** thermometer
9. conducts heat well	**d.** °C
10. slows the loss of heat	**e.** insulation

PROBLEMS

A   B   C   D

1. In each picture, what is used as an insulator? Does it keep heat in or out?

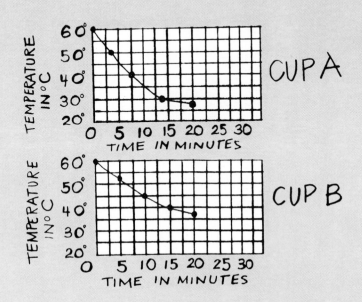

2. Some students put hot water in two paper cups. They put more in one cup than in the other. Then they made these graphs to show how quickly the water cooled. From the graphs, which cup do you think had more water in it? What makes you think so?

3. The two thermometers show the same temperature. But the metal part of the desk feels colder than the wooden part. Why?

FIND OUT on Your Own

1. When you are not sick, the temperature inside your mouth is about 37°C. This is your body temperature. But is it the temperature of your whole body? Find out the temperature of other parts of your body such as:

- your closed hand
- your armpit
- your chin
- the top of your head

2. When a room's temperature is 18°C, how much of the room is really at that temperature? Find out what the temperature *range* (from lowest to highest) is in a room at home. Where is it coldest in the room? Where is it warmest?

9 It All Depends!

Look at the pictures of these living things, or *organisms*.

Look at their names, too.

Which ones do you know?

Moth larva

Poison ivy

Dragonfly

Red-bellied snake

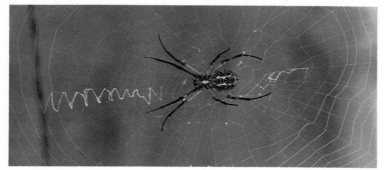
Orb-web spider

Ragweed

SOMETHING TO THINK ABOUT

Write these headings on a paper:

HELPFUL   HARMFUL   NOT SURE

Write the name of each organism under one of the headings. If you don't know an organism, its name may suggest where to place it.

When you have finished, check your list with a classmate's.

On which organisms do you agree?

On which do you disagree?

Crow

Helpful or Harmful

Dragonflies. What stories have you heard about dragonflies, or "darning needles"? Does their name sound dangerous? Names can give you wrong ideas sometimes. Do they look dangerous? Looks can give you wrong ideas, too.

Dragonflies are fun to watch! They may even land on you if you are very still. Don't be afraid! Dragonflies don't bite.

Adult dragonflies eat mosquitoes and some kinds of flies. They catch them in flight!

Dragonfly nymphs. Young dragonflies, called *nymphs,* live in still ponds. They eat small insects, worms, and mosquito larvae. Dragonflies live from one to four years as nymphs. Once they become adult dragonflies, they live only a few more months.

Try to visit a pond or bay with lots of weeds growing in it. Dip a strainer along the bottom near the edge. Try to find a nymph like the one in the bottom picture. Put it in a shallow pan with some pond water and feed it tiny worms. Watch it for awhile before returning it to the pond.

Blackbirds. Blackbirds eat both plants and animals. Sometimes they eat seeds. Sometimes they eat insects.

Suppose blackbirds were feeding in a field. Could they be eating seeds that were just planted? If they were doing this, would the birds be helpful or harmful to people?

Could they be eating insects? These insects may eat plants that people need. If so, would the birds be helpful or harmful to people?

Suppose a blackbird caught a dragonfly. Then, would the blackbird be helpful or harmful?

Is it easy to tell if an animal is helpful or harmful? It all depends.

Dandelions—helpful or harmful? Dandelions can grow in many places:

- in lawns
- in city parks
- on golf courses

They can grow tall or short. They can grow in sunny places or in shady places.

Many organisms eat dandelion leaves or seeds. Some people make soup from dandelion buds. Some make a kind of hot drink from its roots. Others make a salad from its leaves.

Is a dandelion helpful or harmful when it grows in a lawn? Along a roadside? On a bare hillside? On a golf course?

Can a dandelion plant be helpful at one time but harmful at another? How?

SOMETHING TO TRY

Make some dandelion soup. Collect a cupful of dandelion buds before they become flowers. If any yellow color shows, don't use them. Wash the buds well in tap water.

Put them in a pot. Add a cupful of water. Also, add two pinches of salt. Set the pot on a stove or hot plate. **Safety Note:** *Be sure an adult is present.* Boil the mixture for about 5 minutes.

Eat the soup as soon as it is cool enough. How does it compare with other soups that you eat? Are dandelions helpful in this way?

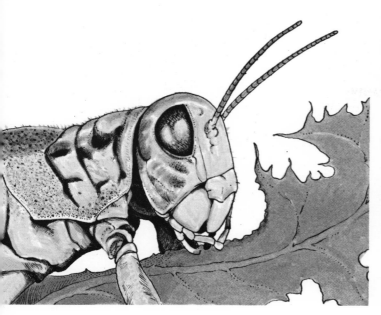

Helpful one time, harmful another! A grasshopper sometimes eats dandelion leaves. It also eats corn leaves.

Suppose a grasshopper is eaten by a spider. Is the spider helpful or harmful? To whom?

What if the dandelion grew in a lawn?

What if you wanted to make soup from its buds?

Does what you think about the spider depend on where the dandelion or the corn grows? Why?

Aphid   Ladybird beetle   Spider

Aphids

Ladybird adult

Aphids are tiny, soft insects that use plant juices for food. When many aphids live on one plant, they may weaken or even kill it.

Adult "ladybugs," or *ladybird beetles,* eat aphids. Their larvae do, too. Are they helpful or harmful to people?

Sometimes spiders eat ladybird beetles. Then, are the spiders helpful or harmful to people?

How do you know if an animal is helpful or harmful? It all depends! In fact, can an animal be helpful at one time and harmful at another?

SOMETHING TO THINK ABOUT

Suppose that aphids suck juice from weeds. Then, what about ladybird beetles? Are they helpful if they eat the aphids?

What about spiders that eat these beetles?

Ladybird larva

Garden spider

210

Louisiana milk snake

Mice and milk snakes. Mice eat corn and other grains that farmers grow. Farmers need the grain for farm animals. Mice live in the fields. And they often live in barns and in farmers' houses.

Mice eat the seeds of many weeds, too. Some of these weeds grow in farmers' cornfields. Some grow along the edge of the roads or lanes.

A milk snake can live on a farm. It is not poisonous. It does not drink milk. It doesn't eat corn and other grains either.

A milk snake does eat mice. It can even climb inside walls to find mice. Is the milk snake helpful or harmful? To whom?

Living Things Compete LESSON 2

Many seeds fell from this tree. Each seed has the soil, water, air, and light it needed to grow.

How many do you think could become full-grown trees? All of them? No, there are too many! They are too close together. As they get larger, there is not enough space, either. So most will not live. Most will never become trees!

It is the same with grass, dragonflies, and spiders. Most organisms produce too many young. Not all can live. There is not enough soil, water, and sunlight for all seeds from all plants. And there is not enough food, water, and space so that all new animals can live.

Living things *compete* with one another for the things they need. They compete for food, space, water, and sunlight. Not all become adults and have more young.

Red maple seeds

Mantises hatching

Eastern milk snake with eggs

Not all survive. A red maple tree produces thousands of seeds. Some land several metres away. But most land near the parent tree. Each one could grow into a full-grown tree. Do you think each one would? In what ways would the new plants compete with each other?

When young praying mantises hatch, they are very hungry. They eat almost any small insect or spider they can find. Often, they eat one another. What do you think happens as they compete for food? How many of these young mantises do you think would become adults? Why?

Soon after snake eggs hatch, the young snakes must find food. When many young snakes all look for food in one place, do they compete? Do you think all of them can find the food they need?

Suppose mantises and snakes both eat the same kind of insect. Do they compete for food? In time what might happen to the mantises and snakes? Why do you think so?

SOME THINGS TO THINK ABOUT

Suppose that hawks lived only on mice. And mice lived only on grain.

1. Would hawks compete with each other for mice?

2. Would mice compete for grain?

3. Could the amount of grain make a difference in the number of hawks? How?

4. Could the number of hawks make a difference in the amount of grain? How?

Competing for food. These are the same kind of larva. They eat the same kind of leaf. They compete with one another for food.

Rabbits are more active at night than in the daytime. They eat leaves and the bark from small trees. They compete with other rabbits for food.

Deer eat leaves, young twigs, and grass. They compete with other deer for this food.

What does "compete for food" mean? Do rabbits compete with larvae for food? Do larvae compete with rabbits? With what animals do deer compete for food? Might deer compete with plants, too? How?

When plants and animals compete, are they helpful or harmful to each other? It all depends.

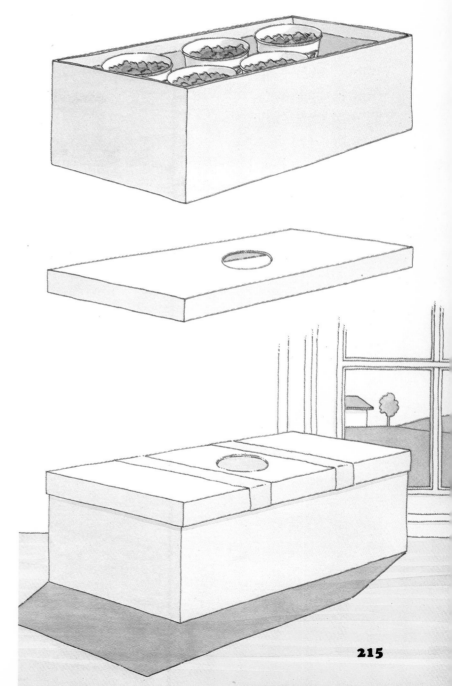

Experiment to see one way that plants compete. Soak some seeds overnight. Fill a cup with soil. Then plant one seed 1 cm deep in the soil. Moisten the soil with water. You will place your cup in a box that you'll share with several of your classmates. To prepare the box, cut a 4-cm hole in the lid. Then cut a piece of wax paper and tape it over the hole. Have each person place his or her cup in the box. Then put on the lid. Set the box in a well lighted place.

Each day remove the lid for only a minute or so. Add a spoonful of water to each cup. Also, observe the growth of the plants. Do this for two weeks. Keep a record. Use it to help you answer these questions:

1. Do the plants grow equally well at first?

2. After several days, what difference is there?

3. What seems to be causing the difference?

People, Control, and Change LESSON 3

Have you seen apples like these? One is beautiful and probably tastes good. The other is not so nice. It may not taste good. What do you think causes the difference in apples?

Apples are used as food by many organisms. People eat apples, but so do many kinds of insects. Also, many kinds of *mold* grow on apples.

To grow apples, farmers must kill organisms that hurt the apples. One way is to spray the apples. The spray kills insects that eat apples. It also kills mold that might grow on the apples. Is spray helpful for people who want apples? Is a farmer who uses spray to *control* pests being helpful?

216

Poison sprays control organisms that compete with people for food. But could the same sprays
- kill some of the food that birds need?
- kill some spiders?
- kill some ladybird beetles?
- kill some things on which a snake depends?

Often, when people control one organism, they are being helpful—to people. But might they be doing harm to other organisms? What happens when people try to kill certain organisms? Can people be helpful and harmful at the same time? In what way?

SOMETHING TO THINK ABOUT

The praying mantis is often called helpful. That is because it eats other insects.

The praying mantis eats insect pests such as flies, aphids, mosquitoes, and grasshoppers. To whom is it helpful when it eats these insects?

Many people think there should be a law against killing the praying mantis. That is because the praying mantis eats beetles that eat garden flowers. But the praying mantis eats many other organisms, too. It eats ladybird beetles, spiders, and sometimes honeybees. It may even eat another mantis! Would such a law be helpful or harmful? Why?

217

Upsetting a community. Do you live in a city or a town? Near a lake or the seashore? All communities are part of one large community—the earth.

People can live on nearly all parts of the earth. Wherever they live, they cause changes. Can you think of any big changes that people have caused near you?

Sometimes the changes that people cause are helpful. Sometimes they are harmful. People do not always know what will happen when they try to control or change things. But before they act, they should think about what might happen.

Once there were no rabbits in Australia. People brought a few rabbits from another part of the world. They set them free.

Many young rabbits were born. There were few other animals that hunted them for food.

The rabbits began to compete with sheep and cows. Before long, it was hard for sheep and cows to find food. Something had to be done. Thousands of rabbits had to be killed.

Upsetting your community. People can cause bigger changes than any other organism. They can change mountains, forests, lakes, or rivers. They can bring in certain organisms and control others.

People can change a community in other ways, too. Sometimes they send harmful chemicals into rivers or lakes. They dump waste into the sea and into the air. Often, people do not think about how their actions can change a community.

People are part of the same community as trees, grass, birds, and insects. People interact with all of them.

What will it be like in your community when you grow up? It all depends! On whom?

Ideas for REVIEW

- Living things we call harmful are not always harmful to people.

- Living things we call helpful are not always helpful to people.

- There is not enough food, water, soil, and space for all young living things to survive.

- Living things compete with each other for the things they need to survive. Not all become adults and have more young.

- When plants and animals compete, they may be helpful or harmful to one another.

- People can control many organisms that compete with people for food.

- In controlling pests, people often kill other organisms that they don't really want to kill.

TEST Your Understanding

A. On a piece of paper, write the word or words that make each sentence correct. *Do not write in this book.*

1. When two organisms try to get something that is not enough for both, they _____ for it.

2. A farmer sprays crops in order to _____ the insects that eat them.

3. People can bring a new _____ into a country where it never lived. But they must think about what it might do when it gets out of control.

4. A poison spray is helpful when it controls pests, but _____ if it kills organisms that aren't pests.

5. The organism that can make the biggest changes in a community is _____ .

B. On a piece of paper, copy the words just as they are below. Then draw arrows between each pair of organisms in this circle that depend on each other in some way.

human

earthworm
grass

maple tree
apple tree

dandelion
mouse

cat
spider

sunfish
dragonfly

mosquito

PROBLEMS

1. Write down or draw the changes that would happen in a community if
   - a new parking lot were put in a park.
   - a dump were leveled and planted with grass.
   - a dam were put on a stream near a city.

2. This swamp is being changed to another kind of community. Why do you think some people would want to change it? Why do you think some people would not want to change it? If it were up to you, what would you do with the swamp?

FIND OUT on Your Own

1. Look at these organisms and their names. Can you tell by looking whether each is helpful or harmful? What would you have to know to tell? How could you find out?

2. Look in a mirror. Who do you see when you look into it? In what ways is that person a very important person in any community? Think about this on your own. Then share your ideas with your teacher and classmates.

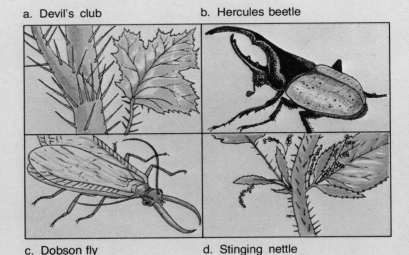

a. Devil's club   b. Hercules beetle

c. Dobson fly   d. Stinging nettle

Glossary and Index

The pronunciation is given for each word listed in this glossary. The stressed syllable in a word appears in capital letters.

The list below shows you how to use the symbols in the glossary to pronounce words.

Letter	Example	Spelling	Letter	Example	Spelling
a	cat	KAT	i	him	HIM
ah	Brahms	BRAHMZ	ī	kite	KĪT
ar	car	KAR	o	dog	DOG
ay	say	SAY	ō	hole	HŌL
e	hen	HEN	oo	moon	MOON
ee	meet	MEET	or	for	FOR
er	her	HER	u, uh	sun	SUN
g	grass	GRAS	z	zebra, runs	ZEE-bruh, RUNZ
j	jam, gem	JAM, JEM	sh	she	SHEE
k	kiss, cat, quick	KIS, KAT, KWIK	th	think	THINK
s	so, cent	SO, SENT	zh	measure	ME-zher

carbon dioxide (KAR-bun dī-OK-sīd). a heavy, colorless, odorless gas that is part of the air, 10.

cartilage (KAR-tuh-lij). the substance often found where two bones meet. Cartilage helps to protect bones, 110.

Celsius (SEL-see-us). a scale on a thermometer. 0°C is the freezing point, and 100°C the boiling point of water, 188.

community (kuh-MYOO-nuh-tee). a group of living things that live together and interact, 12.

compress (kum-PRES). to squeeze or press something, such as air, into a smaller space, 98.

conductor (kun-DUK-ter). something through which heat, sound, or electricity can move easily, 195.

contract (kun-TRAKT). to draw together or become smaller. Both muscles and air can contract, 114, 182.

decay (dee-KAY). to break up, waste away, 5.

depend (di-PEND). to rely on, to need, 7.

dissolve (di-ZOLV). when something mixes with a liquid and disappears, 24.

expand (eks-PAND). to spread out, to become larger, 182.

fair test (FAYR TEST). an experiment in which only one thing is tested at a time, 8.

graph (GRAF). a picture that shows how one thing compares with another or how one thing changes in relation to another, 192.
gravity (GRAV-uh-tee). a force that tends to draw objects toward the center of the earth, 60.
grid (GRID). evenly spaced lines or dots often used for locating things, 81.

insulator (IN-suh-lay-ter). something that does not let heat, sound, or electricity move through easily, 195.
interact (in-ter-AKT). to act on one another. Things that interact affect one another, 5.

joint (JOYNT). the place where one moving bone is joined to another, 110.

location (lō-KAY-shun). where something is, 80.

mass (MAS). the amount of matter in something, 55.

opaque (ō-PAYK). blocks light, 141.
organism (OR-guh-nizm). a living thing—plant or animal, 204.
oxygen (OKS-suh-jun). a colorless, odorless gas that is part of the air, 10.

relax (ree-LAKS). loosen up; what happens when muscles stop pulling, 115.
rib cage (RIB KAYJ). a kind of cage formed by the breastbone, ribs, and backbone; it protects the lungs and heart, 107.

sample (SAM-pul). a part of something that shows what the rest is like, 190.
scale (SKAYL). *1:* marks evenly spaced along a line and used for measuring, 42; *also 2:* an instrument used for measuring the pull of gravity on something, 60.

skull (SKUL). the bones of the head; it protects the brain, 106.
spinal cord (SPĪ-nul KORD). the cord that runs through holes in the vertebrae. It carries signals between the brain and other parts of the body, 106.
standard (STAN-derd). something that is always the same no matter where it is used, 41.

thermometer (ther-MOM-uh-ter). an instrument for measuring temperature, 182.
translucent (trans-LOO-sunt). lets some light through, but cannot be seen through clearly, 141.
transparent (trans-PA-runt). lets a lot of light through and can be seen through clearly, 141.

unit (YOO-nit). an amount of something. A standard unit is an amount that is always the same, 44.

vertebra(e) (VER-tuh-bruh, VER-tuh-bray). each bone in the backbone, 106.